Genealogical Research

in Nova Scotia

Terrence M. Punch

PETHERIC PRESS LTD.
Halifax, Nova Scotia, Canada
MCMLXXXIII

Copyright 1978

Terrence M. Punch

ISBN-0-919380-29-8

Third Edition 1983
Third Edition, second printing 1985

Published by

Petheric Press
Nimbus Publishing Limited
P.O. Box 9301
Station A
Halifax N.S. B3K 5N5

Contents

INTRODUCTION

More than thirty years have passed since R.M. Hattie read his paper about genealogy in Nova Scotia to the Nova Scotia Historical Society. He concluded his address in November 1951 with a plea for people to get interested in Nova Scotian genealogy. His paper was published by the Society in volume thirty of its **Collections** in 1954 and then, if the printed page be the criterion, nothing happened for above a dozen years. In 1967 the Public Archives of Nova Scotia issued its brief (13 pp.) pamphlet, "Tracing Your Ancestors in Nova Scotia". A revised and enlarged (17 pp.) version of this leaflet appeared in 1976. At the request of the Nova Scotia Museum, late in 1975 I prepared an Info bulletin entitled "Find Your Family" (9 pp.). Until 1978 this is the sum and substance of genealogical guide writing in the province. Some general genealogy books have had sections which treated of Nova Scotia, but the number of pages written exclusively about material in this province does not exceed one hundred, and some at least of these were done by non-residents or as part of something more sweeping in scope.

During the past several years there has been an active genealogical association within the Royal Nova Scotia Historical Society. It has produced workshops and publishes **The Nova Scotia Genealogist** which has grown into a magazine in all but name. Its success in reaching those doing family tree research in Nova Scotia has created a large flow of correspondence, much of it conveying basic information. People have developed a desire to find their forebears, but for want of any comprehensive guidebook they are obliged to pepper the handful of genealogists in the association with questions that could often be resolved if there was a source of reference. In short, a need exists for an up-to-date guidebook to Nova Scotian genealogical material.

Hoping to fill this gap, the author and the publisher discussed the state of affairs and decided that what was most required was a book that would be inexpensive, portable, and yet encompass sufficient material to be authoritative in its field. This short book has some general genealogical lore within it, but this has been held to a minimum. The main means of combining completeness with brevity has been to ignore sources outside Nova Scotia. Except for a few Acadian references in Moncton, everything mentioned in this guide may be found within Nova Scotia. There is more here than I am free to mention, such as the private compilations of local genealogists who may be willing to help the occasional inquirer, but who are not about to turn themselves into branches of the Public Archives. The local history societies may help you to locate such kind souls. This book should help you to learn a good deal of information without bothering anyone. Such is my hope. Happy hunting and good luck!

ACKNOWLEDGEMENTS

In undertaking to compile a guide such as this one, an author is under a sense of obligation to everyone who has laboured in the vineyard before him, and it is probable that any attempt to single out everyone who has assisted me will fail to include all of them. So rather than run that risk, I will acknowledge that I have been helped with ideas and suggestions from many people in many places, including the staff of the Public Archives of Nova Scotia, the several local historical societies, assorted church bodies, fellow-members of the Genealogical Committee of the Royal Nova Scotia Historical Society, and the dozens of family historians who have asked my advice in the past several years. To all of these folks, my sincerest thanks for their encouragement and helpful advice.

— Terrence M. Punch, 21 October, 1978

Genealogical interest and activity has enjoyed a phenomenal growth since the first edition was written in 1978. Now, we in the Maritimes are on the verge of further breakthroughs in the area of genealogical standards and professionalism. This third edition retains and expands somewhat the material which we had from Stephen White of the Centre d'Etudes Acadiennes, Moncton, whose assistance has been as gratefully received as it has been generously given.

Thanks to Elizabeth Eve, who put many hours of intelligent work into making this edition the best one yet. A further debt is owing to other executive members of the Genealogical Association of Nova Scotia for the hints they have dropped in conversation, and to John Spearns, an especially sharp-eyed student in one of my classes in Atlantic Canada Studies at Saint Mary's University, who found 'typos' where others missed them. Finally, my thanks to my wife and family whose consideration has allowed me to devote the time to this project. Dated at Armdale on the birthday of the youngest.

— T.M.P., 28 May 1983.

I — GETTING STARTED

Why Bother?

Do you know who you are? Of course you do. You are Margaret Jones or Louise Boudreau or Karen O'Brien or Harry Lucas or somebody with a name. Unless you've been adopted as an infant or have discovered that your parentage is beyond your discovery, you know your parents' names too. This is reassuring. The process of gaining the deep security of your identity is even better when you know who your grandparents are, or were. If you met your grandparents and listened to their voices and perhaps to their stories, you must feel a snug memory that is very much a part of yourself.

The time that your Newfoundland grandma got all steamed up and went and sat in the corner behind the stove in her rocker and drew on her dudeen (clay pipe); the day your Cape Breton granddad told you about his first day as a boy down in a pit, sweating his first piece of coal out of a seam; the night your Lunenburg granny scared you in front of the fire with tales of ghosts and second sight; the trout you and granddad caught together and fried over a fire in the woods; these are memories to treasure. If you and I can experience that sort of closeness to our forebears, we can count ourselves blessed and lucky.

Thousands of our people cannot recall the intimacy of a grandparent or perhaps even of a parent. Yet, I believe that there is in every human soul a basic need for that ultimate sense of belonging that comes from feeling part of a continuing lifeline which starts somewhere back in the remote past. The twentieth century is a period of rootlessness, a time when so many people live away from their place of origin, away from Home, away from themselves.

A century ago, the Annapolis farmer knew who he was and what he had come from. He could take you back of his field and show you the mounds and perhaps the stones over them. "There's my granddad, and over there's his father who came up here from down the States after the French Acadians were put out." If pressed, he might get out the great family Bible, where two or even three generations of people had written in hands firm or

1

shaky the names of their children. Here you might have seen that "Sukey was delivered of a girl child at 5 in the morning of July the 7th, in the year 1805." He might show you the apple trees his father had planted the year King William died. Your farmer might even know that this sort of tree was planted because Bishop Inglis or Squire Prescott had recommended the type. But, the man knew who and what he was.

We poor twentieth century nomads live in a world that has largely lost its grip on its own past. I once asked a classroom of schoolchildren how many of their parents were natives of Halifax and vicinity, and only about half of the class had one Nova Scotian-born parent. This situation is not at all unique. Job opportunities and improved transportation have encouraged great numbers of people to move once or many times during their lives.

Whatever the explanation, people have recently begun to acquire a renewed interest in their personal heritage. Every weekend floods of family historians visit archives and libraries, cemeteries and church offices in search of their elusive ancestors. Each summer hundreds of expatriate Nova Scotians or their children and grandchildren return to the ancestral turf to find their ancestry. A good general name for all of this digging and delving is genealogy.

Genealogy is the art or science of tracing and recording the family relationships of people. It is an art in that it is concerned with human beings within an historical context, and it is a science in that it does proceed along lines of hypothesis and conclusion, deductive reasoning, and has its own peculiar terminology. As a record of the human past of living people, it forms a most vital part of our community and individual heritage.

There are probably many reasons, some simple, others complex, why people become interested in genealogy. There was long a barrier to the pursuit of genealogy in many people's minds because there was fear of being considered a snob for concerning oneself with such things. Today that road block has been removed from our thinking processes and genealogy is seen for what it always has been, or should have been: the means by which the individual family can find its past and its share in forming the heritage of the community in which it lives or used to live. Very few people trace their ancestry today in hopes of proving a relationship to a long-vanished prominent personage. For one thing, such people came to see that being descended from some historical worthy made no difference to anyone. Your friends were already your friends, and your enemies weren't any more likely to clasp you to their bosoms because your fifteenth great-grandfather had turned out to be a lord.

Today's genealogist is concerned with everyone's ancestry, and not just with that of the aristocracy. A run of forebears who were cabinetmakers or jewelers, shipwrights or stonemasons, farmers or mariners is every bit as valuable and valid as would be a tenuous connection to a long-vanished earl

2

or a pilgrim. And possibly more desirable, since there was an apposite remark made to me some years ago by a learned and experienced clergyman that many of the original bigshots had been merely successful robbers. This is not written to disparage genuine noble descents, but to suggest that genealogy as a search for reflected glory does not impress knowledgeable people.

There is a good numbers exercise to try sometime, which will show the basic silliness of doing genealogy to find the famous forebear. All you have to be able to do is to multiply by two. We each have two parents, who each had two parents, who each had two parents, and so on. If there were an average of three generations to a century, twenty-three generations should bring you to the period when Magna Carta was signed (1215). If you have been multiplying by two those twenty-three times you should now have a figure of 8,388,568 people as your potential maximum number of ancestors alive at that time! Cousins do marry, and distant cousins married quite a lot. To allow for that cut the figure by two thirds. You still have about three million forebears alive at the time when King John was putting his signet upon the seal. That is enough forebears to include John, all the barons present (and, who knows, maybe a bishop or two), all of the peasants for miles around, and quite a throng of others. Does it really matter that you or I can trace a line back to King John, unless we accept that there may exist another quarter million lines that we cannot trace because everyone in them was a peasant before 1500?

What do we do, then? We look for names and dates and places. We try to connect them one to another in logical and demonstrable relationships or family trees. We also attempt to find out what sort of people our ancestors were. What did they look like? What did they do in their daily lives? What sort of events affected their community while they lived? For instance, it would take a very unthinking researcher to trace his family back to someone who lived in Boston between 1765 and 1776 and who would not wonder what effect the American Revolution had on the man. Did it make him a Loyalist? What caused him to leave Boston? Did he express an opinion about events, an opinion which came down in family tradition or in a letter? These things matter.

Genealogy, then, is a broad and interesting field, a kaleidoscope of our human past, a spectrum of what we have been. It involves the finding of information, the assembling of facts into patterns of relationship, the weighing of evidence, the holding of interviews, the writing of letters, the filing of information, and the presentation of the findings either in print or in a family history. It concerns the dedicated genealogist in the fields of history, demography, geography, foreign languages, heraldry, and paleography, to name but a few. Your legal and mathematical knowledge will get a workout. It is an exciting field, and each person may decide how far he or she can or will go. Take up the challenge, fellow Bluenoser. I don't think you will regret it.

3

Getting a System

When I was a boy there used to be a hardware store in Halifax. It claimed with some justice to have everything from a needle to an anchor. If you could bring the genial proprietor away from a discussion of politics or the price of cars, and put your request to him, he would smile and disappear. Generally, his voice floated in from the back of the store to tell the customer, "We've got one. I saw them around here just the other day!" Sure enough, five or twenty-five minutes later, he would come in, gleefully holding the required washer in his hands and say that would be two cents. It was a dreadful waste of time and, in retrospect, I am chilled to think of the possibilities that store offered to shoplifters. That storekeeper was well liked, but his lack of a system was wasteful in every way. If there is a lesson in all of this, it is that the genealogist ought not to operate like that hardware dealer. Find a method that you like and follow it. If you cannot come across one, invent one of your own. Every experienced genealogist has his or her own personal ways of keeping track of their work.

There is a dazzling variety of choice on the market today for the family historian to choose from. Every other publisher and genealogical group seems to offer ancestry charts, family history sheets, ancestral fan charts, work sheets, etc. Personally, I like index cards and large pieces of paper which can be punched and carried around in loose-leaf binders. A quantity of lined loose-leaf paper or foolscap is also handy. If you like to go first class, then by all means go and buy a collection of commercial forms for family research. But don't let anyone take your money on the grounds that such printed stuff is indispensable, because it is not. Use of a coherent system of keeping your notes is crucial; using any one kind of forms is not.

The mechanics of recording your family tree information will vary with the type of printed or self-designed forms you are using. A number of very useful general guidelines will give you all the necessary instruction. For the present, let's look at a few things to do or not to do.

Record in pencil any facts that are open to challenge, or which need proof or verification. That way you can ink over the pencil if the information is correct and thereby save the trouble of rewriting a chart or a page. If your first information proves erroneous, you can change it readily. Leave lots of room when you are recording. Write on every second line if necessary, so that you will have more room to make insertions as you learn more details, e.g., a middle name, or a more exact date ("7 May 1905" instead of "after 1904").

One useful practice to adopt is that of writing dates in the sequence: number of day, name of month, number of year — e.g., 17 June 1878. After all, you may know that your "10/9/03" means 10 Sept. 1903, but if someone else had written it could you be sure it was not 9 Oct. 1903 or even 1803 that was intended? If you find a date recorded "10/9/03" the context will in most cases provide the year for you, but until you find the month and day you will be wise to copy it as you found it, putting it in quotations marks and follow it with the source in parenthesis: "10/9/03" (date of Mr. Smith's letter to grandfather telling him his brother had died the day before).

Use women's maiden names, since most records trace male lines of descent and almost every published genealogy is essentially patrilinear (father-to-son) in its format. Also, most women appear in records in conjunction with their husband or father, so it keeps marriage alliances more visible to the reader if you express women's names in their maiden form.

You should strive for three types of recordings of your discoveries. These will be family group record, a narrative history, and an ancestry chart. The first tells the names and events, dates and places, of a man and wife (or wives), and their children's names and births. The second gives biographical details about each head of a family group and his wife. The third allows a ready reference to see what part of your ascent needs to be explored next.

The word **ascent** reminds us that many lineage seekers do a double research job on their family. We work to **ascend** the family tree to the earliest knowable generation, then we **descend** the tree to trace the branches. If we get back to our great-grandfather's father, John Macdonald, 1798-1876, of Inverness County, and then bog down on getting further with his Scottish forebears, we can work forwards towards ourselves by trying to trace all of John's descendants. If this family remained small, we can hope for completeness. If the clan spread prodigiously, you can keep busy for years tracing them down, and enjoy the dozens of new kinsmen you meet and hear from. Either way, it will be satisfying.

Some Things to Watch For

Those who do genealogy are often confused by their findings. Approach any record with caution and be sure you are copying it correctly and as fully as you will require. Remember also that what you see written or typed in a record may be in factual error either because the information was originally supplied in a false or mistaken form, or because of a clerical error at the time the reocrd was made or subsequently copied.

There are several built-in hazards to which we can succumb if we do not learn how to get around them, and then remain on guard against mistakes. Let's examine a few things that tempt genealogists into forming mistaken interpretations: vocabulary, calendar, handwriting, and changes of name.

The **vocabulary** of words used to describe family relationships in older wills and other documents does not match current practice in many respects.

5

A "cousin" could have been almost any relative except a parent or child. The word has been applied to nephews, brothers-in-law, grandnieces, etc. So when you read of two people being "cousins" allow for other interpretations of the word than the common one of our time.

The method of describing cousins by number causes endless confusion and it is as well to explain this problem now and save some people from unnecessary trouble. There are two methods and they do not agree beyond first cousins on terminology. The legal and ecclesiastical system numbers cousins by the number of generations the persons are removed from siblings. The children of two brothers are therefore first cousins. The grandchildren of two brothers would be second cousins, and so on. The relationship between a person and his first cousin's child would be that of first cousin, once removed. The common system used by many people agrees with the foregoing as to first cousins, then departs sharply in vocabulary. The child of a first cousin is called your second cousin. Your children are your second cousin's third cousins, and so on. It is all very confusing until you get used to it, but you should at least know there are two methods in use, the one proper, the other informal but commonly used.

Perhaps an example will help to explain the two systems. Let us say that Arthur Ferguson and John Green are first cousins, and that each has a son. Arthur's son would be the second cousin of John's son, according to the church and the law. But, many people in speaking will say that Arthur is the second cousin of John's son, and that Arthur's son is the third cousin of John's son. According to Law and

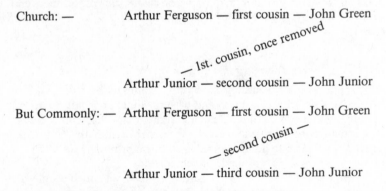

Church: —   Arthur Ferguson — first cousin — John Green

— 1st. cousin, once removed

Arthur Junior — second cousin — John Junior

But Commonly: —   Arthur Ferguson — first cousin — John Green

— second cousin —

Arthur Junior — third cousin — John Junior

A century ago a son-in-law or a daughter-in-law might have been a stepchild rather than the spouse of one's daughter or son. A "natural child" until about 1840 may mean a child born to oneself as opposed to the child of one's spouse by a former marriage. When our ancestors meant an illegitimate child the word "spurious" was often used as a descriptive term.

We accept "senior" and "junior" as referring to a father and son, but years ago people could refer to any two men in one community who happened to have the same name. Thus we should not assume that such men were father and son. We must allow for the possibility of uncle and nephew, kinsmen, or even two totally unrelated individuals within a relatively small area. A remarkable error of this kind was made in Nova Scotia where many sources treated Hon. Michael Tobin Sr. and Jr. as father and son, whereas they were, in fact, an uncle and a nephew.

For many family historians, the **calendar** supplies further problems. The calendar in general use in the western world is the Gregorian version, which was adopted by Pope Gregory XIII in 1582. Protestant nations such as England and some German states refused to accept a "Catholic" calendar. This stubbornness persisted until 1752 by which time the Julian calendar was eleven days behind the Gregorian. Britain decided to change over to the reformed calendar in 1752, and her colonies, including Nova Scotia, followed suit. The day after 2 September 1752 was counted as 14 September.

Another idiosyncracy of the old calendar was to begin the year from 25 March ("Lady Day" or "Annunciation Day"). When some people started counting the year from 1 January, it became necessary to write dates between then and 25 March as a double year — e.g., 14 February 1749/50, which meant it was 1749 by Julian, and 1750 by the Gregorian, reckoning. That was better for us than the earlier practice wherein 28 February 1739 was in fact eleven months **later** than 28 March 1739. It is the helpful practice of some authors to tell which system they are using by placing the abbreviations **O.S.** and **N.S.** after dates. **O.S.** (Old Style) means that the Julian calendar applies, and **N.S.** (New Style) signifies the use of the Gregorian calendar.

We can make a quaint error if we find, for example, that Elisabeth Rothenhauser died 17 April 1785, aged 72 year 5 months and 6 days at Lunenburg. We subtract and find a birthdate of 11 November 1712, give or take a day. But has the burial record allowed the eleven days? Did the German state where she was born follow the Julian or the Gregorian calendar? The change began in Protestant German states about 1700, but took nearly a generation to become universally accepted. Prudence dictates that you give her death date with age at death, unless you have another source for her date of birth to clarify the matter. And just be sure then that the other source is not derived from this same burial record.

The third problem area centres about **handwriting.** Perhaps the most frequent source of trouble is the long **S,** which was much used until about 1810 both in print and in writing. It is easy to confound **S** with **F** or even with **P** in such handwriting. This practice began to diminish from about 1800, although as lately as 1850 you will find the long **S** still being used among the self-educated and the elderly. Letters **I** and **J** were indexed together in many old books and in some cases a small **J** appears where today we'd use an **I**.

Some Lunenburg records (e.g., early Lutheran church registers, some wills) were written in German and the script is deceptive. You should not rely on your own interpretation unless you know German or have had long practice with the script. Canon E. Harris's abstracts of names form a partial but fallible guide to locating entries in the Lutheran registers. The author has made a translation of these records for 1772-1797, baptisms and marriages, and a copy may be consulted in the Public Archives of Nova Scotia (reference M.G.1. Box 1487).

Should you feel confident enough to try, here is a German alphabet in the script much used in the 18th. century. Just keep in mind that handwriting has personal idiosyncracies, whatever the script.

A,a 𝕬,𝖆	B,b 𝕭,𝖇	C,c 𝕮,𝖈
D,d 𝕯,𝖉	E,e 𝕰,𝖊	F,f 𝕱,𝖋
G,g 𝕲,𝖌	H,h 𝕳,𝖍	I,i 𝕴,𝖎
J,j 𝕵,𝖏	K,k 𝕶,𝖐	L,l 𝕷,𝖑
M,m 𝕸,𝖒	N,n 𝕹,𝖓	O,o 𝕺,𝖔
P,p 𝕻,𝖕	Q,q 𝕼,𝖖	R,r 𝕽,𝖗
S,s 𝕾,𝖘𝖙	T,t 𝕿,𝖙	U,u 𝖀,𝖚
V,v 𝖁,𝖛	W,w 𝖂,𝖜	X,x 𝖃,𝖝
Y,y 𝖄,𝖞	Z,z 𝖅,𝖟	ss ß

Linked to handwriting is the old habit of abbreviation. The syllables **tion** or **sion** are sometimes collapsed so that "occasion" is written **occasn**. The family historian must note names with especial care. A few common examples noted in records in Nova Scotia include:

Abm. = Abraham	Geo. = George	Thos. = Thomas
Bart^W. = Bartholomew	Hy. = Henry	Wm. = William
Chas. = Charles	Jas. = James	Xpher. = Christopher
Fred^k. = Frederick	Jno. = John	Xtiana. = Christiana.

A wholesale copyist such as Canon Harris was hurrying to get everything, so he wrote his own shorthand. **J** meant John, **M** meant Mary, **Mar** meant Margaret, **Mag** meant Magdalen, and so forth. Partly one must come to know the record he/she is using, and partly one must know something about the matter before plunging in.

A fourth problem area is that of **name changes**. Beginners in family tree research are vague to the point of total innocence with regard to the wide, even wild, variety of spellings for almost any name. There are people who would shed blood over a name having **Mc** or **Mac** as a prefix. **Mac** is Gaelic (both Irish and Scots) for "son of", and it is often abbreviated to **Mc**, or even to **M'** as in M'Apline. The idea of **Mac** being Scottish and **Mc** being Irish has no legal or linguistic sanction whatever. Of courses, Dr. Thomas McCulloch of Pictou was a Scot, but by the faulty logic of the "McMac" tribe he must be assigned to the Irish. Nor does the business of a capital or a small letter in a **Mac** name signify much. It is purely a convention in some families used to distinguish a MacLean from a Maclean of another derivation. Today people may know the difference, but it is doubtful that many of the poor Highlanders coming over in 1790-1840 knew the correct spelling of the names, and they had fierce family and clan pride. Had they felt an insult they'd have been quick enough to say so.

There is no name I have seen that cannot be spelled in a variety of ways, some obvious and others almost unrecognizable. Take into consideration further that some people took other surnames to get an inheritance, bury a foreign-sounding name, or to escape a past misdeed. The name Punch looks straightforward, yet it is a much transformed name. Starting 800 years ago as Pons, it has been variously Poins, Poyns, Pointz, Ponz, Pounche, Ponson, FitzPons, Punce, Ponce, and many other things before reaching its present form. There are three existing variants — Punch, Poyntz, Pounch. Just to keep it good clean fun for the genealogist, three branches have adopted entirely different surnames, and have become Clifford, Golden, and Harrington. Fifteen years of work and many discoveries later, I know this, but when I began I had not an inkling of what to expect. Nor is this a unique example.

Names become distorted in several ways. The person himself may not have known the proper pronounciation of his name, so that anything could have been written in a record without the man being any the wiser. Secondly, people frequently mispronounced names and wrote them by ear. Beaulieu became Bellew in such a fashion. Regional accents do wondrous things to names, while translation can disguise LeBlanc as White, Casey as Quessy. Written records, of course, perpetuate original errors and pronunciations that were written by ear.

Pseudo-translations or anglicizations are really noticeable among the names of the Lunenburg settlers who got labelled "Dutchmen" by their Anglophone contemporaries. Considering that the Lunenburgers were nearly all Germans, Swiss, and Montbeliardians, to call them "Dutch" seems but to symbolize the casual, even careless, way in which the English majority noted their individual names. The chance for error among such people's names was very great. Take a mass of German-speakers, many of them illiterate or from areas with no settled surnames, to Holland. Have Dutch-speaking clerks record their name. Pass them over to English petty officialdom and put them down on the Atlantic coast of Nova Scotia, where "anglicizing" and faulty translations would soon complete the process begun up the Rhine three or four years earlier. The result was chaotic spellings. Why should

Johann Heinrich Seiler's grandchildren be named Sawler, and those of Johann Michael Seiler be named Zeller? What logic prompted some part of a family to become Hirtle, and another part Hartling and Hartlen?

If you want to trace your Lunenburg ancestor in Europe, you have not only to find the town or district or origin overseas, but also to determine what name you are seeking. Ask for Isnor and you may not get help, but seek Eisenhauer or close variants and perhaps you'll do better. Here is a sampling of twenty Lunenburg names under **one** modern and **one** 18th. century spelling:

Now	Then	Now	Then
Awalt	Ewald	Leslie	Laessle
Barkhouse	Berghaus	Longard	Lankert
Clattenburg	Klettenberger	Nieforth	Neufahrt
Corkum	Gorckum	Publicover	Bubickhoffer
Cook	Koch	Rafuse	Rehfuss
Creaser	Krüser	Ritcey	Henrici
Deal	Thiel	Slaunwhite	Schlagentweit
Haverstock	Oberstahl	Turple	Törpel
Heisler	Haussler	West	Wüst
Hilchie	Uelsche	Young	Jung

French Lunenburgers from Montbéliard had just as many changes, for example: Bigney was Biguenet; Countway was Comptois; Dorey was Dauré; Grono was Grosrenaud; Jollimore was once Jollimois; Perrin had been Jeanperrin; while Rhyno or Reyno reached this country as Renaud. Seek all the variants of your name and consider the possibility that there may have been a translation or adaptation over the years. Names have not been as sacrosanct as some guardians of the vestal virgins would have us believe.

A book could be written to tell about all of the pitfalls that await the unwary. We have looked at a sampling of four common traps that can easily ensnare us. Before moving along, there is one other point to mention. The average family counts three or four generations per century. If you get a family that does not do so, it may be merely an unusual lineage, but it also may be a case of "lost generation." When common names appear for both husband and wife in two successive generations of a family, it can be all too easy to lose one of the generations if insufficient data can be found to allow ready distinctions to be made.

Here is an example. John "X", born 1800, married 1822 Susan, b. 1804, and had John, b. 1823, and eight others, b. 1824-1839. Then William was born in 1844 and Robert in 1846, sons of John and Susan "X". Children of the first couple? This did seem quite likely until a marriage record dated 1843 was found for John, bachelor, and Susan, spinster. Even then, you cannot be sure of the parentage of William and Robert. If you found a death record of the older Susan in 1840, you'd be getting somewhere, provided that the 1843 marriage record was not mistaking John, bachelor, for John, widower. If you find the death record of the older John in 1840, you would be shed of the mystery. In the case upon which this specimen is based, the matter was not clarified until the wills of the two Johns, father and son, had been examined. Then the will of one mentions two sons named Robert and William and the other does not. Moreover, the date of probate indicates that the senior John died sometime in 1844. But, I hope you can appreciate how readily a generation of that family could have become lost.

On this note of caution let me conclude this brief discussion of pitfalls. Be at all times a thorough detective, a full-time historian, a snoop, and a keen observer, as well as a hardened skeptic. At times you will need to be a linguist and a lawyer as well. But don't let my caution scare you. I'm posting a SLOW sign, not a STOP sign.

Within The Family Circle

In genealogy the tried and proven best method is the logical one. We work from the known to the unknown. We start with ourselves, then we work back to our parents, then to our grandparents, and so on into the past.

You ought to find out everything you can from your own resources and the family circle **before** ever you go near a records repository or a hired genealogical searcher. You can approach these persons and places too soon and, in an unprepared state, make yourself more of a nuisance than anything else. You can get much more information than you think, and I believe that you will be pleasantly surprised to see what is, or could be, in your house or in that of your close relatives.

There are three stages in this preliminary research. These include a document hunt, an interviewing and letter-writing phase, and a publicity possibility. Let's look through these things one by one.

In the widest historical sense, a document can be anything that tells us something about the past. It need not be a piece of paper, although usually that is what is intended by users of the word. We will start with these commoner types and work towards the more unusual. The **family Bible** or large old prayer books frequently had a page or pages in which a family record could be entered. Here were entered the births, marriages and deaths of family members. Check the date of the Bible, so you can tell whether the entries were contemporary with events or written in from memory years later. The closer the record to the event, the better its chances of accuracy. If all entries are written in the same handwriting and appear to have been entered in one bunch, you must assume that all of the entries except the most recent have to be either written from memory or copied from an older

11

record. In both cases there is a chance for error that would not have existed when an entry was made at the time of the actual event.

Old letters and **diaries** are important sources of clues, although events in a letter are often described with a wealth of detail that may not advance your search (e.g., the bride wore a white gown). However, such description may flesh out the family history when you want to lend truthful colour to your finished presentation of your research, so note the details and where you found them. **Photo albums** and **scrapbooks** don't just tell us that Uncle Eben was a shutterbug, or that Aunt Clara liked to save the frilly edges off of greeting cards and put them in her scrapbook. Pictures, with or without captions, provide much information. They are a great way to break the ice if you are interviewing someone you do not know very well, because you can get them talking about who this one or that one was. In scrapbooks you may well find one of several excellent genealogical clues: memorial cards of the deceased (often with the date shown), newspaper clippings (let's hope the clipper thought to copy the date of the events, otherwise you will have some information with no idea of just when the events took place), and possibly even birth or marriage certificates.

When you were a youngster or teenager, did you ever go through a period after Christmas or your birthday when you chased all your relatives and friends to get them to write you verses because you had a new **autograph book?** These little books may provide you with twenty novel endings to "Roses are red and violets are blue", but they occasionally turn up things of importance, since it was the practice of those giving autographs to write the date. You just might find something like this: "Happy birthday, Robbie, on your 19th birthday, from Aunt Harriet, November 10, 1917." If you didn't know Robbie's birthdate, you have an excellent clue now. If you didn't know he had an Aunt Harriet, you have now to look at his parents' siblings for possibilities, as well as who married his uncles. Then too, "Aunt Harriet" could have been a sort of honorary rather than a literal aunt. I had an "Aunt Jean" for years, who turned out to be my mother's cousin, but we children always spoke of and to her as an aunt.

Although class **yearbooks, report cards, and school pictures** may not get us very far into the past, they can provide their share of clues if we study them. Another item which was once quite common, but which today is a thing of the past, is the **tester.** Young girls made these exemplars of their skill with the needle and they were put up in the family sitting room as a discreed advertisement to young gentlemen that the young woman could crochet, stitch, knit or sew. Not infrequently, these testers would bear a full name and date of birth. Other documents that might turn out to be helpful would be old **ration books,** framed **certificates** from lodges or training institutions, and dozens of other things whose discovery is limited only by our imagination and our ancestors' ingenuity.

12

During or after your document hunt you will need to speak to others in the family and seek their help. If the relatives live handy and you have kept in touch with them, it is quite an easy thing to drop in or call up and ask for their help: "What was Aunt Mary's maiden name?"; "Did Joe's two boys both go to Maine?" But what if the relative is a distant, perhaps unknown to you except that this person in Oklahoma is the widow of your grandfather's younger brother, and is presumably the only living person who knows your great-grandfather's name? Then you must write letters, unless you can afford the time and money to go out to Oklahoma to visit the lady. Keep a record of what you ask in your letters, so that if you are writing several people, you can remember what you asked of each, and will not annoy them with repeated requests. Also remember to send a self-addressed stamped envelope (SASE in advertisements) if your correspondent is in Canada, and a self-addressed envelope with an International Reply Coupon if they live outside Canada. Keep letters of request to the point, polite, and don't ask too much at once. Offer to pay postage both ways if you borrow any papers, then copy them promptly, and send them back in A-1 shape. And always write to say "thank you."

When you have gone through all of the papers, Bibles, clippings and photos that you can lay hands on in the recesses of your own home and those of your kin, you should stop and write it all down in order. Reflect carefully upon what you have collected, and decide what are the next steps to be taken, the next gaps to be filled. You may well be ready to begin interviewing.

It is very important to select the correct person to whom to talk. The human element as a resource is very fragile. If you delay talking to your most elderly relations, you may never talk to them. Plan accordingly, and try to talk as soon as possible with those whose help may not be available in a few years. The oldest ladies are the best prospects for rewarding interviews, since the women of their generation were more intimately part of the family grapevine than were the men. Men tend to recall genealogically useless items such as the fact the Cousin Alvin from Grand Rapids drove down in a Model A in 1928, and to forget that Alvin's wife was named Joan, or that they had three children with them. Decide to whom you should turn and arrange an interview. The first step in taking action is to make an appointment and to keep it.

Be sure you go to the meeting with all you will need. If you wish to tape the interview, be sure to ask their permission to do so. If they agree, well and good, but if they refuse, then you must satisfy yourself with using pen and paper. Talk for a while first, so that the older person can see that you are really interested and know what you are talking about. One genealogist visited an elderly lady for help. She turned out to be very informative, but not until she had told him all about his cousin Eldon who kept interrupting her, and in the end she had packed Eldon off with a flea in his ear! Our genealogist is still holding his tongue.

Remember that however keen and clear their memory, older people are like the rest of us. If they can have time to think about a question, they may well remember more and give you a better answer. Do not hustle the elderly citizen for answers. Most of us cannot tell upon demand the full names and dates of birth of all four of our grandparents. Yet some people expect an 88-year-old who is getting deaf to rattle this off like a computer. Patience and diplomacy pay dividends.

To get started in an interviewing session, you might take a chart with you that will allow you to show what you know so far. Or take along a few pictures of relatives that may be recognized by the interviewees. When you get talking, ask specific questions. If you come in and say to them: "Tell me all about your family", can you be too surprised if the magnitude scares them into silence or generalities?

Some examples of specific questions might be these: "What was your grandmother's maiden name?"; "Do you know who has the old family Bible?"; "Dad says you and he had an Uncle named Ralph. What happened to him?"; "Did your grandparents come up to Halifax to live, or did they stay down in Guysborough?"; "Mother once told me you were named Sarah after your grandmother. Which one was she?"; "What church did your family go to?"; "Did the family have a private cemetery, or did they bury in the churchyard?"

Variations of these and other questions can produce information. Some interviewers come up against the problem of information that does not check out. If you know from reputable sources that something was so, and now your interviewee is contradicting that fact, what should you do? My advice is to keep quiet at the interview and take down all of the information as given. Then go back to your source — a document or a newspaper clipping — and re-examine it carefully. Can it be reinterpreted in such a way that it agrees with the version given by your informant? If it can, then I'd be inclined to accept the interviewee's version if it is to do with something within his or her own experience. If it cannot be reconciled, you must decide either to regard the matter as less certain than you had thought, or to go back to your interviewee and, when a suitable chance arises, feed in the other version to them. This should be done in a casual way and not flung out like a challenge. It is a good way to dry up a source or to start a fight by more or less calling them a liar or a forgetful old dotard! Better to let it alone if on the second occasion they stick to the version given previously. Chances are that you will find some other means to corroborate one version or another later in your research. The important thing is that it is far better to have two accounts rather than none at all. At least you will have some

14

specific points to investigate. For instance, if a newspaper clipping said a lady who died in 1845 was named Mary Ann Brown, and her granddaughter, now 90, says the name was Margaret, you should be able to find something somewhere that will support one version or the other: a deed, a will, a church record, a Bible entry. If your informant's version was correct, it would be nice to tell them that they were. If they were incorrect, does it matter? By checking further you have established the fact more firmly than before. Let that be its own reward.

There is another thing to remember about interviewing those who are very frail or elderly. Two or three short visits may be better for the older person than would be one marathon session. They may like the opportunity to talk about times when they were younger and more active. They may also enjoy the attentions of a visitor, and may ration out their information just so you will come back again. People do like to feel useful and necessary, and many elderly folks don't often get the chance to have that feeling. Be patient and willing to come again. It does no harm to bring a small gift or to send a "thank you" note afterwards. If they read or knit or play cribbage or collect something, it might be nice to give them a book or some yarn or candy or whatever might make them feel appreciated and happy.

One person that I know got some information from a distant relative in the metropolitan Halifax area. The interviewee was one of an elderly couple in an older house. The interviewer and his son went over the Saturday morning after the interview and mowed the lawn, weeded an overgrown flowerbed, and replaced several fence pickets as a way of saying "thank you." Need I say that they were rewarded with a lovely lunch and the invitation to come and talk about the family any time? It does no harm to make friends with people; it reduces the sense some interviewees may have of being used. Good luck with your interviews. May you find your acquaintances as pleasant as they will find you.

There is a third preliminary step you may wish to try. That is publicity. An advertisement can be placed in newspapers asking if anyone knows the whereabouts of relatives of X.X., who lived in Parrsboro from about 1898 to 1937, and then moved to Ontario. If some relatives are located in answer to this advertisement, then you may write to them or interview them. If that tack fails, you can try to place a more specific advertisement or query in a genealogical magazine. As we'll see later, there is such a magazine in Nova Scotia. There are dozens of others in almost every state and province, the services of which can be had for very reasonable charges.

When you have accumulated, investigated, sorted, classified, arranged, studied, understood and doubted all the contents of your house, your relatives' houses, Grand Aunt Susie's memory, and ten letters or so, you are ready to put down a rough working chart of the family tree. This exercise will pull it together for you, as well as indicate just where the next points of attack should be. You are ready to pass along from the phase of "getting started" to the stage of "getting somewhere." As a rein on the reckless, and as a caution to us all, let's take a quick look at some of the logic of researching family trees.

Evidence

Evidence is a body of information that tends to prove or disprove the truth of something. It is anything that can help us in reaching valid conclusions. The newer genealogist ought to recognize that there are not only varying degrees of reliability in evidence, but also different levels of certainty about conclusions.

The extent to which you can rely upon a source of information is obviously an important consideration. When two or more sources conflict in their presentation of "facts", it helps to be able to decide how much weight to give each source. As a general rule of thumb, prefer a primary to a secondary source. Each time a record has been transcribed, the possibility of simple human error enters the picture. If you can look upon the actual church marriage register, it is better evidence than a marriage date culled from a printed county history. If you can examine the actual will rather than an abstract, do so, for it is more credible. The contemporary record (one made at the time of the event) is preferable to the retrospective record (one made some time afterwards). A written source for a very old fact is generally more reliable than is a verbal tradition.

Any record is only as good as its source. It does no harm to be skeptical and ask yourself who created the record and to what purpose. An unimpeachably genuine petition for a land grant may be written by a man who was extenuating his circumstances in order to get the most he could. One case I've studied was that of a man seeking land. His request mentioned that he had eleven children. That was the literal truth, but he failed to add that four of the eleven were married and no longer dependent upon him, nor that two others were dead. At a time when each dependant could mean an additional fifty acres of land, it was a severe temptation to many to exaggerate to their own advantage.

A good distinction to make in your evidence is that between proof and clues. Here are some examples to show what I mean. Birth date recorded at baptism is **proof** that a child was presented and baptised, and was presumably of about the age recorded. It is a **clue** that the child may have been born on the date recorded as that of birth, and a **clue** that the child of such-and-such a name was born to certain parents. A marriage record is **proof** of a marriage, of the names used by the parties, and (in most cases) of their marital status. It is a **clue** to the ages and parentage of those married. A

16

death record proves that a person of a certain name died on a date and in a place specified, but offers only a lead to age and parentage.

Bible entries should be proof, but be sure that the entries were made contemporaneously with the events. Check the date the Bible was published against the entries. A Bible printed in 1853 that records births from 1791 and 1793 can be taken as giving a **clue,** but certainly not as proving the dates for you.

Cemetery records are proof that someone was buried and suggest an approximate date of death, but only indicate name, age or birthplace of the deceased. Further evidence is needed to prove these things. Census returns are usually proof that the persons listed lived at that date and place, but can hardly be taken as more than clues to age, origin or birthplace.

Leads, but not proof, can be gathered from oral tradition, newspaper notices, and passenger lists. These sources are more apt to be distorted or garbled than they are to be wantonly misleading, and in most cases are reasonably accurate. However, another corroborating piece of evidence is desirable. All of this is not to induce in you a haunted feeling that past record keepers have conspired to hide the facts. It is just that the accumulated experience of dozens of genealogists is that old records were not kept as competently as they might, and that copyists make errors. Being copyists ourselves, we know that the most alert of us is human and fallible.

It is legitimate to deduce from and interpret your sources in order to get at the facts. For instance, you might know that John (1837-1911) and Henry (1838-1899) were brothers, but you do not know their parentage. You learn that John was naturalized in the United States in 1869, had a service file from the Civil War, and a death certificate in 1911. All three agree on the names of his parents. You may justly proceed on the assumption that John's parents were also Henry's.

You have an adult couple named Blaney in a remote area. Church records gave the baptisms of children born in 1842, 1844, 1847 and 1849, of that surname. All but the 1844 entry give the parents' first names. You can fairly take it that the 1844 entry is probably part of the same family, inasmuch as the overwhelming weight of evidence supports that deduction. Dull as it may sound, most of the time things did (and do) take place in the most obvious way. The most reasonable explanation is usually the correct one. Bear in mind, though, that sometimes there will be a strange conclusion to your evidence. Deduce, but do it with a fair measure of caution.

So far we have been talking about getting started. Now let's turn our attention to getting somewhere. Psychologically prepared and somewhat organized, you are ready to get out and search for information beyond the family circle. And for all this seriousness and caution, do try to enjoy your research. Keep a sense of humour and an optimistic outlook, but stay alert and be prepared to use your ingenuity.

Select Bibliography of Genealogical "How-To" Books

This is neither an exhaustive list, nor is it intended to recommend one book over another. Many other competently written books are on the market, but they are not well enough known to me to discuss them. All the titles here should be available for purchase, and certainly you will find many of them in a good bookstore or in the local library. Anything published before 1960 has not been included.

For a Canadian family historian perhaps the following five books represent an ample cross section of genealogical literature:

Baxter, Angus. **In Search of Your Roots: A Guide for Canadians Seeking Their Ancestors.** Toronto: Macmillan of Canada, 1978. Very complete, written at a professional level.

Fellows, Robert F. **Researching Your Ancestors in New Brunswick, Canada.** Fredericton: Public Archives of New Brunswick, 1979. What you need to know to search in New Brunswick.

Gregoire, Jeanne. **Guide du généalogiste, à la recherche de nos ancêtres.** Montréal: Guerin, 1974. Second edition of book first written in 1957. The best French-Canadian guidebook.

Jonasson, Eric. **The Canadian Genealogical Handbook.** Winnipeg, Wheatfield Press, 1978. When you want to see what provinces beyond Quebec have to offer.

Jones, Orlo. **Family History in Prince Edward Island.** Charlottetown: P.E.I. Heritage Foundation, 1981. A genealogical research guide to the Island province.

Morris, Julie. **Tracing Your Ancestors in Nova Scotia.** Halifax: Public Archives of Nova Scotia, 1981. A useful introduction to the Public Archives.

Four British books that are useful are the following:

Genealogists Handbook. London: Society of Genealogists, 1969. A short guide to using records in the British Isles. Excellent value.

Iredale, David. **Discovering Your Family Tree.** Aylesbury: Shire Publications Ltd., 1973. Inexpensive book for beginners in British research.

Mander, Meda. **Tracing Your Ancestors.** Newton Abbot, England: David & Charles, 1976.

Matthews, C.M. **Your Family History.** London: Butterworth Press, 1976.

The big output of recent genealogical instruction comes from the United States. Those which I found informatively written by people of wide family seeking experience are these:

Doane, Gilbert H. **Searching for Your Ancestors.** Minneapolis: University of Minnesota Press, 1960 (3rd ed.). Proof that genealogy was not invented by Alex Haley.

Helmbold, F. Wilbur. **Tracing Your Ancestry.** Birmingham, Alabama: Oxmoore House, Inc., 1976. The author is an expert librarian, genealogist and teacher.

Williams, Ethel W. **Know Your Ancestors.** Rutland, Vt.: Charles E. Tuttle Company, 1960.

An entertainingly different approach is taken in a book by Suzanne Hilton, **Who Do You Think You Are?** (Philadelphia: The Westminster Press, 1976). The authoress brings a welcome sense of cheerfulness and enjoyment to her genealogical quest. The British genealogist L.G. Pine, in **American Origins.** (Garden City, N.Y.: Doubleday & Company, Inc., 1960), offers a very useful volume for those who want to take their ancestry back to locations outside North America. Pine, in **The Genealogist's Encyclopedia.** (New York: Collier Books, 1969), brings this up-to-date but in less detail than the 1960 book.

Finally there is the ultimate evidence that genealogy has become truly a popular North American hobby. The February 1978 edition of the **Consumer Guide,** out of Skokie, Illinois, is entitled "Tracing Your Roots." It is an interesting collection of information, which will appeal to some readers, if not to everyone.

Doubtless many another book and pamphlet will be generated in response to the current genealogy boom, and there may be some that are excellent and which I have not listed. Please treat this bibliography merely as some suggested places to turn for guidance, and not as the last word on the subject. Browse in a bookstore or library and find a book that suits your level of interest and experience. Choose one that you consider interesting and attractive. When you have digested it, get one or two more and form a synthesis of the several approaches. But do not become a scholar of one book, for there is no such thing as the Bible of Genealogy.

II — GETTING SOMEWHERE:
THE PRINTED PAGE

Like baseball, genealogy requires you to warm up before beginning to play. By now, the enthusiastic beginner will have talked the ears off all of his elderly and not-so-elderly relatives, exhausted the family Bible, turned the attic and closets upside down, and corresponded about his family tree with other people. You have been doing a preliminary survey of what is available on the home front. Now, however, your notes have started to grow thick and your knowledge of the family is a little deeper than it was when you commenced. You can see what details you need to check out, and what you ought to try and discover. Do the verifications first, because you require as many valid leads as possible before setting off on an ancestor-hunt. Today, Nova Scotia is your search area, but tomorrow you could be writing for information from anywhere on earth.

Let's proceed to look over the types of records you will find when you venture into a library or an archives. You already know how to read the library index cards so that you can find books on the shelf. They often do not tell you all that you had hoped, and I find that usually if I copy the call numbers for three or four books on a subject in which I am interested, I will find related books on the adjacent shelves. If you experience any difficulty, help is as handy as the library desk, where a trained person is available to help you, and they may sometimes make useful suggestions as to what to try. Since libraries specialize in secondary, and archives in primary sources, let's begin this discussion of records by making clear the distinction between primary and secondary records. You are acquainted with secondary material, since books, magazine articles and newspapers fall into that category, and most literate people use these things often enough to be familiar with them.

A **primary source** is one that was created at or near the time and place of the events it describes. A participant, such as the clergyman, writes down the baptism or the burial. The witnesses sign the will. The teacher lists her pupils in the school register. Primary records are generally immediate ones, with nobody standing between the event and the record of the event, and they are much more desirable than secondary sources by their very nature of being contemporary records, created by a participant or an eye-witness to events. The primary source is not infallible; folks do forget details, mistake names, or wait too long to write down the information which forms the written evidence — the document.

A **secondary source** is someone's interpretation of what happened, or a copy that has been made from an original document. A written history book or thesis is an interpretation, and not a mere chronicle of events. That one fact necessitates care on the part of the reader of such works. Authors draw selectively upon their material. For instance, a good source of information is a physical map of a community, showing every house and the name of the occupant. A geographer may ask how many people lived in the valleys, and how many on hillsides, and evaluate his data in correlation with soil studies. A sociologist may ask which income groups lived where, and try to see if the community was grouped into "classes" residing in areas according to wealth. An educator may look to see where a school could be placed to advantage. You can see the point that the presentation will reflect the questions which were addressed to the evidence. Likewise, each author has his way of seeing things. There is nothing "wrong" with that, but you should know and accept such legitimate biases.

Secondary sources form a great mass of material held in the average library. Despite their shortcomings, such books and articles have great potential value for you, the family researcher. They are the reasonable starting point for you when first you begin to take your research to libraries and archives.

Local Histories

There are a great number of county and local histories about the various parts of Nova Scotia. Some, such as Eaton's history of Kings County, contain appreciable genealogical compilations. Others, such as Campbell's history of Yarmouth, do not present genealogies at all. Many books, especially older ones, lack comprehensive indexes, and in recent years some have had indexes compiled by those interested in the particular county history — e.g., Smith's index to Wilson's history of Digby County; Marble's index to Miller's history of Colchester County. Some of the local histories are badly written, monstrously prejudiced, or cry out for the hand of an editor. Some have one author, educated and erudite; others have been written by members of a church group or a women's institute. Some are venerable and come from a Victorian pen; others are as recent as last week. The publications in the field of local history are a spectrum of quality, ranging from the excellent to the trifling. Yet, the genealogist cannot risk bypassing anything in print on an area in which he has an interest. There is often a nugget of pure genealogical gold buried in the debris of a rambling dissertation upon a community or a county. These books and pamphlets afford much useful information and whatever one thinks of any particular book or its author, one reads through the material patiently and hopefully. Sooner or later, you will learn something of value, either about your particular family, or at any rate about the community/county in which they lived.

The following is a listing of some local histories, arranged by county. Within each, the general county histories are given first, followed by the several community histories within each county. This is not a list of every history written about a Nova Scotian community, but a guide to the better part of those histories which are available in the libraries around the province. Libraries in each area will probably have more complete holdings for their particular region of the province, including unpublished or mimeographed material produced by schools, clubs, and local groups of various kinds.

NSHQ stands for the **Nova Scotia Historial Quarterly; NSHR** for the **Nova Scotia Historical Review;** while **NSHS** refers to the **Collections** of the Royal Nova Scotia Historical Society.

ANNAPOLIS COUNTY
County
Calnek, William A. **History of the County of Annapolis,** 660 pp., 1897.
Savary, Alfred W. **Supplement to the History of the County of Annapolis,** 142 pp., 1913.
Local
Comeau, J.A. **The Oldest Parish in Canada: On the Catholic Parish of Annapolis Royal, N.S.,** 59 pp., 1962.
Coward, E.R. **Bridgetown, Nova Scotia, its History to 1900,** 253 pp., 1955.
Henderson, J., comp. **A Compilation of Some History of the Lawrencetown Circuit of the Methodist Church . . .,** 66 pp., 1965.
History of Lawrencetown, 40 pp., 1977.
Irvin, John, "History of Bridgetown", **NSHS,** XIX, 1918.
Kendrick, Mary F. **Down the Road to Yesterday. A History of Springfield . . .,** 141 pp., 1941.
Lawrencetown United Baptist Church History, 1873-1963, 79 pp., 1963.
Leonard M. **Historical Sketch of the Paradise-Clarence United Baptist Church, 1810-1960,** 20 pp., c 1960.
Morse, W.I. **Gravestones of Acadie . . .,** 110 pp., 1929.
_____. **Local History of Paradise, Annapolis County, Nova Scotia (1684-1936),** 65 pp., 1937.
_____. **Supplement to the Local History of Paradise . . .,** 79 pp., 1938.

Perkins, C.I. **The Romance of Annapolis Royal, Nova Scotia,** 121 pp., 1934, 1952

Sutherland, I.M. **Clements Township; its History and its People, 1783-1870,** Acadia thesis, 190 pp., 1957.

ANTIGONISH COUNTY
County

MacDonald., J.W. **History of Antigonish County,** 58 pp., 1975.

MacLean, Raymond A. **History of Antigonish,** 2 vols., 1976.

Rankin, D.J. **History of the County of Antigonish,** 390 pp., 1929.

Local

Inglis, R.E., "Lochaber, a Typical Rural Community," NSHS, XXXIX, 1977.

MacDonald, H.H. **Memorable Years in the History of Antigonish,** 223 pp., 1964.

175th. Anniversary of St. Peter's Parish, Tracadie, N.S., 96 pp., 1978.

Whidden, David G. **The History of the Town of Antigonish,** 209 pp., 1934.

CAPE BRETON COUNTY
County

Brown, Richard. **A History of the Island of Cape Breton,** 473 pp., 1869, reprinted 1979.

Local

Gillis, R. **Stray Leaves from Highland History** (Grand Mira), 43 pp., 1918.

Gray, H.M. **Sydney, a Gateway to Canada,** 23 pp., 1941.

Jackson, E.E. **Windows on the Past: North Sydney, Nova Scotia,** 230 pp., 1974.

McArel, Elinor C. **A History of the Parish of St. Mary's (Glace Bay),** 39 pp., 1976.

MacKenzie, Archibald J. **History of Christmas Island Parish,** 167 pp., 1926.

MacKinnon, J.G. **Old Sydney; Sketches of the Town and its People in Days Gone By,** 143 pp., 1918.

Rankin, D.J. **Souvenir, Old Home Week held at Grand Mira, C.B.** 34 pp., 1916.

Women's Institute. **A Brief History of Mira Gut, 1745-1968,** 40 pp., 1968, 1975.

————. **History of Modern Louisbourg 1758-1958,** 184 pp., 1858.

COLCHESTER COUNTY
County

Creighton, S.F. **Colchester County: a pictorial history,** 176 pp., 1979.

Hamilton, A.M. **A History of Colchester County from the Earliest Times to 1835,** Acadia thesis, 188 pp., 1954.

Miller, Thomas. **An Historical and Genealogical Record of the First Settlers of Colchester County,** 400 pp., 1873.

Ormond, Douglas S. **The Roman Catholic Church in Cobequid, Acadie, 1692-1755, and Colchester County ... 1828-1978,** 340 pp., 1979.

Local

Burrows, Mildred P. **A History of Wittenburg. (St. Anns) ...** , 80 pp., 1978.

Campbell, G.G., "Fort Ellis, Colchester County" **NSHS,** XXIII, 1936.

Crowe, E.M., ed. **The Town of Stewiacke, Nova Scotia,** 137 pp., 1967.

Deyarmond, E.M. **The Whip-Handle Tree (Stewiacke),** 117 pp., 1970.

Longworth, I., "History of the Township of Onslow, Nova Scotia," **NSHS,** IX, 1895.

Murphy, J.M. **The Londonderry Heirs: a Story of the Settlement of the Townships of Truro, Onslow and Londonderry,** 147 pp., 1976.

Patterson, Frank H. **A History of Tatamagouche,** 143 pp., 1917.

Stephens, David E. **Truro, Railway Town,** 88 pp., 1981.

University Women's Club. **Cobequid Chronicles: a History of Truro and Vicinity,** 111 pp., 1975.

Women's Institute. **Bass River Village History,** 91 pp., 1955.

_____ **A History of Beaver Brook,** 75 pp., 1959.

_____ **The Story of Five Islands, Colchester County,** 132 pp., 1969.

_____ **History of Great Village, Nova Scotia,** 155 pp., 1960.

CUMBERLAND COUNTY

County

Grimmer, F.D. **The History of Cumberland County,** Acadia thesis, 129 pp., 1951.

Local

Bird, Will R. **A Century at Chignecto, the Key to Old Acadia,** 245 pp., 1928.

Bowser, Elaine, et al. **A Profile of the Tantramar Marshes,** 132 pp., 1978.

Brown, Harry R. **The Valley of the Remsheg,** 255 pp., 1973.

MacNab, A.M. **The Pioneers of Malagash, Genealogical Record from the Early Days,** 68 pp., 1952.

MacQuarrie, John R. **Malagash Salt,** 112 pp., rev. ed., 1981.

Milner, W.C. "Records of Chignecto," **NSHS,** XV, 1911.

Scott, Bertha. **Springhill, a Hilltop in Cumberland,** 119 pp., 1926.

Smith, James F. **The History of Pugwash,** 378 pp., 1978.

Trueman, Howard T. **The Chignecto Isthmus and its First Settlers,** 268 pp., 1902.

DIGBY COUNTY

County

Wilson, Isaiah W. **A Geography and History of the County of Digby,** 471 pp., 1900.

Local
Bull, Mary Kate. **Sandy Cove, The History of a Nova Scotia Village,** 188 pp., 1978.
Centenaire de la Mort du Père Jean-Mandé Sigogne, 64 pp., 1944.
Clayton, Hazel. **Smith's Cove and her Neighbours,** 2 Vols., 1961, 1962.
Deveau, J. Alphonse. **Along the Shores of St. Mary's Bay,** 2 vols, 1977, 1978.
Deveau, J. Alphonse. **LaVille Française,** 286 pp., 1968.
Eglise Saint Bernard, 104 pp., 1942.
Greenwood, Walter R. **History of Freeport, Nova Scotia, 1784-1934,** 46 pp., 1934.
Heritage Remembered — the Story of Bear River, 174 pp., 1981.
Hill, Allan M. **Some Chapters in the History of Digby County and its Early Settlers** 115 pp., 1901.
Kitto F.H. **Maxwellton District, Nova Scotia; a new area for settlement in an old settled province,** 44 pp., 1924.
Powell, Robert B. **Scrapbook: Digby Town and Municipality** 106 pp., 1968.
_____ **Second Scrapbook: Digby Town and Municipality** 117 pp., 1973.
Wade L.D. **Historic Glimpses of Picturesque Bear River, Nova Scotia,** 34 pp., 1907.

GUYSBOROUGH COUNTY
County
Hart Harriet C. **History of the County of Guysborough,** 290 pp., 1877.
Jost, Arthur C. **Guysborough Sketches and Other Essays,** 414 pp., 1950.
Local
Cooke, Findlay. **History and Stories of Issac's Harbour and Goldboro,** 231 pp., 1976.
Franchville, Edith E.W. **History of the Parish of Guysborough,** 1950.
Hart, Harriet C., "History of Canso, Guysborough County, Nova Scotia", **NSHS, XXI,** 1927.
Jost, A.C., and J.A. Morrison. **Historic Canso,** 63 pp., 1928.

HALIFAX COUNTY
County — none.
City
Akin, Thomas B. **History of Halifax City,** 272 pp., 1895.
Blakeley, Phyllis R. **Glimpses of Halifax, 1867-1900,** 213 pp., 1949, 1973.
Clairmont, D.H., and D. Magill. **Africville: The Life and Death of a Canadian Community,** 272 pp., 1974.
Raddall, Thomas H. **Halifax Warden of the North,** 343 pp., 1948, 1971.
Local
Along the Shore (Petpeswick to Tangier), n.p., 1982.
Around the Harbours (Jeddore), 2 vols., 1981.

Bayer, C.W. **Christ Church, Dartmouth, Nova Scotia, 1817 to 1959,** 165 pp., 1960.

Campbell, Margaret Kuhn. **A Tale of Two Dykes; the Story of Cole Harbour . . . ,** 67 pp., 1979.

Handforth, E., et al. **This is Waverly, Nova Scotia,** 40 pp., 1960.

Hartling, Philip L. **Where Broad Atlantic Surges Roll,** 243 pp., 1979.

Lawson, Mrs. William. **History of the Townships of Dartmouth, Preston and Lawrencetown,** 260 pp., 1893.

Lowe, Winnifred. **History of Moser's River and Other Stores** 50 pp., 1978.

Martin, John P. **The Story of Dartmouth,** 550 pp., 1957.

Meade, Gary G. **History of St. James Anglican Church, Boutilier's Point . . . 1846-1981,** 41 pp., 1981.

Mullane, George. **Footprints around and about Bedford Basin,** 46 pp., 1912.

Payzant, Joan & Lewis. **Like a Weaver's Shuttle; a History of the Halifax-Dartmouth Ferries,** 214 pp., 1979.

Punch, Terrence M., "The Estates and Haunts of Dutch Village", **NSHQ,** 1975 supplement.

Regan, John W. **Sketches and Traditions of the North West Arm,** 181 pp., 1909, 1978.

Rutledge, James E. **Sheet Harbour: A Local History,** 108 pp., 1954.

Smiley, Mrs. B.G. **Historical Recordings of Beaver Bank, 1898-1968.**

Taylor, G.H. **Early Days and Pioneers of Musquodoboit,** 22 pp., 1948.

Tolson, Elsie C. **The Captain, the Colonel and Me (Bedford, N.S., since 1503)** 164 pp., 1979.

Vernon, C.W. **The Story of Christ Church, Dartmouth . . . ,** 219 pp., 1917.

HANTS COUNTY
County

Draper, T.F. **History of Hants County,** unpublished manuscript, P.A.N.S., 1881. (A.E. Marble's index is available at the P.A.N.S.)

Local

Aitken, W.E. **St. David's United Church, Maitland. Hants Co., N.S.** 41 pp., 1968.

Anslow, Florence **Historic Windsor . . . ,** 32 pp., 1962.

Brown, Pearl A. **Rambling over the Roads and Hills of Newport Township,** 124 pp., 1967.

————. **The Story of Cinq Maisons and Georgefield,** 257 pp., 1976.

Caldwell, M.A. **The Nine Mile River Church: Now and Then,** 53 pp., 1969.

Chittick, H. **Hantsport, the Smallest Town,** 46 pp., 1940, 1964.

Duncanson, J.V. **Falmouth - A New England Township in Nova Scotia** 474 pp., 1965, 1979.

Hind, Henry Y. **Sketch of the Old Parish Burying Ground at Windsor, N.S.** 99 pp., 1889.

Mosher, E. **North Along the Shore**, 124 pp., 1975.

Pope, William. **Portrait of Windsor; the Wonderful World of Windsor, Nova Scotia**, 49 pp., 1965.

Ross, J.A. **The Story of Newport Township**, 22 pp., 1932.

Shand, G.V. "Windsor, a Centre of Shipbuilding", **NSHS, XXXVII**, 1970.

_____ **Historic Hants County**, 168 pp., 1979.

Thirkell, F.W. **The First Two Hundred Years: The Story of the Parish of Newport and Walton**, 107 pp., 1959.

Wallace, Mrs. Ernest, "The History of the Municipality of East Hants," **NSHQ, VIII, 4**, 1978.

INVERNESS COUNTY
County

MacDougall, John L. **History of Inverness County, Nova Scotia**, 690 pp., 1922.

Local

Bird, Lillian S., "My Island Home", **NSHQ** (Dec. 1975) (Port Hood Island).

Chaisson, Anselme. **Chéticamp: Histoire et Traditions Acadiennes**, 317 pp., 1961, 1972.

Genealogical History, St. Mary's Parish, Glendale, N.S. 99 pp., 1977.

Hart, John F. **History of Northeast Margaree**, 158 pp., 1963.

LeBlanc, Jean-Doris, **Cheticamp, its Pioneers**, 13 pp., 1981.

MacDonald, A.D. **Mabou Pioneers**, 2 vols., n.d. & 1977.

MacNeil, S.R. **All Call Iona Home 1800 to 1950**, 1969.

Smith, Peter W. **History of Port Hood and Port Hood Island**, 276 pp., 1967.

Thomas, George C. **Margaree**, 54 pp., 1980.

A View of the Whycocomagh Congregation, 48 pp., 1956.

KINGS COUNTY
County

Eaton, Arthur W.H. **History of Kings County, Nova Scotia**, 898 pp., 1910.

Ferguson, M.G., and M. McLellan **A History and Geography of Kings County**, 113 pp., 1967.

Kirkconnell, Watson. **Place-Names in Kings County, Nova Scotia**, 39 pp., 1971.

Local

Cox, I.**Bits of History of Canning, N.S.**, 1940.

Eagles, Douglas E. **A Genealogical History of Long Island (North Grand Pré), Kings County, Nova Scotia**, 111 pp., 1977.

_____ **A History of Horton Township, Kings County, N.S.** 37 pp., 1975.

Eaton, Ernest L., "The Survey Plan of Cornwallis Township," **NSHR, I, 2**, 1981.

Lloyd, Olive H. **A History of Prospect in the County of Kings, Nova Scotia,** 83 pp., 1975.

Phillips, A. **A History of Bishopsville, Kings County, Nova Scotia, 1710-1974,** 32 pp., 1974.

Quinn, Edythe. **A History of Greenwich,** 108 pp., 1968.

Rand, J.E. **Historical Sketch of Church of St. John, 1810-1960, and the Parish of Cornwallis, Nova Scotia, 1760-1960,** 1960.

Women's Institute of N.S. **Grist from the Mills: A History of Sheffield Mills,** 118 pp., 1967.

_____ **"The Port" Remembers; the History of Port Williams . . . ,** 256 pp., 1976.

LUNENBURG COUNTY
County

Bell, Winthrop. **The "Foreign Protestants" and the Settlement of Nova Scotia,** 673 pp., 1961.

DesBrisay, Mather B. **History of the County of Lunenburg,** 585 pp., 1870, 1895.

Local

Bolivar, H.K. **History of Conquerall Mills, Lunenburg County, N.S. 1806-1974,** 48 pp., 1975.

Harlow, A., ed. **The Story of Bridgewater, Nova Scotia,** 32 pp., 1967.

Hirtle, W.W. **A Study of Mahone Bay, Nova Scotia,** 55 pp., 1951.

History of Bridgewater, 32 pp., 1967.

Kaulback, Ruth. **Historic Saga of Leheve (LaHave).** 105 pp., 1970.

Lacey, Laurie. **Ethnicity and the German Descendants of Lunenburg . . . ,** 28 pp., 1982.

Langille, B.K. **And Now We Remember, History of Barss Corner, Lunenburg County,** 218 pp., 1974.

Leopold, C.B. **The History of New Ross,** 61 pp., 1966.

Levy, George E. **The Diary of Joseph Dimock,** 208 pp., 1979 (Marriages by this Baptist Minister, 1794-1845, included).

Levy, Herman D. **A History of Sherwood in the County of Lunenburg,** 89 pp., 1953, 1975.

Women's Institute of N.S. **History of Chester, 1759-1967,** 165 pp., 1967.

PICTOU COUNTY
County

McLaren, George. **The Pictou Book,** 267 pp., 1954.

MacPhie, John P. **Pictonians At Home and Abroad . . . ,** 232 pp., 1914, 1915.

Patterson, George. **History of Pictou County,** 471 pp., 1877 (Robert Kennedy's 102 pp., index of proper names in Patterson is available at the P.A.N.S.)

Sherwood, Roland H. **Pictou Parade,** 114 pp., 1945.
Local
Bain, Janet C. **The History of Hopewell, Nova Scotia,** 80 pp., 1977.
Bliss, Edwin T., "Albion Mines, Pictou County," **NSHS, XXXIX,** 1977.
Cameron, James M. **About New Glasgow,** 203 pp., 1962.
―――――――. **More About New Glasgow,** 313 pp., 1974.
Gordon, George L. **River John; its Pastors and People,** 152 pp., 1911.
Grant, Robert. **East River Sketches, Historical and Biographical . . . ,** 92 pp., 1895.
Hawkins, Marjorie M., et al. **Gairloch, Pictou County, Nova Scotia,** 164 pp., 1977.
The History of St. Columba Church, Hopewell, Nova Scotia, 1820-1970, 52 pp., 1970.
MacQuarrie, John R. **Lansdowne (Battery Hill, Wilkins Grant, Upper New Lairg) Sketches,** 44 pp., 1975.
Mawdsley, Lee. **A History of Merigomish,** 93 pp., 1972.
Murray, John. **The Scotsburn Congregaton, Pictou County, Nova Scotia,** 161 pp., 1925.
Reid, Leonard M. **Sons of the Hector,** 64 pp., 1973.
Ross, D.K. **The Pioneers and Churches; the Pioneers and Families of Big Brook and West Branch, E.R. . . . ,** 239 pp., 1957.
Women's Institute of N.S. **A'gleann boideach** (=Beautiful Valley; Bridgeville), 56 pp., 1967.

QUEENS COUNTY
County
More, James F. **The History of Queens County,** 250 pp., 1873.
Local
Dexter, Lucius D. **History of Brooklyn,** 60 pp., n.d.
Long, Robert J.**Liverpool in History,** 44 pp., c. 1911.
McLeod, Robert R., "Notes Historical and Otherwise of the Northern District of Queens County", **NSHS, XVI,** 1912.
Morrison, James H., and L.M.B. Friend, "Queens County Klondike", **NSHQ, IX,** 2, 1979.
―――――――. **"We Have Held Our Own"; the Western Interior of Nova Scotia, 1800-1940,** 159 pp., 1981.
Mullins, Janet E. **Some Liverpool Chronicles,** 296 pp., 1941.
Tupper, F.F. **Historical Liverpool,** 208 pp., n.d.

RICHMOND COUNTY
County — none
Local
Campbell, P.J.M. **Highland Community on the Bras d'Or,** 151 pp., 1966.

SHELBURNE COUNTY
County

Robertson, Thomas. **Akins Historical Prize Essay on Shelburne County,** MS. in P.A.N.S., 1871.

Local

Archibald, Mary. **Gideon White, Loyalist,** 68 pp., 1975.

Crowell, Edwin. **A History of Barrington Township and Vicinity, Shelburne County, Nova Scotia, 1604-1870,** 603 pp., 1923.

Doane, Frank A. **Old Times in Barrington,** 95 pp., 1948.

Freeman, Ruth H. **My Branch of the Descendants of Ralph Smith: A Genealogy with a Brief History of Barrington and Cape Sable Island, Nova Scotia,** 33 pp., 1975.

Nickerson, C.E. **A History of Cape Sable Island, Shelburne County, Nova Scotia,** 1946.

Perry, Hattie A. **In and Around Old Barrington,** 103 pp., 1979.

Perry H. **This Was Barrington,** 119 pp., 1973.

Richardson, Evelyn. **My Other Islands,** 213 pp., 1960.

Robertson, Marion. **King's Bounty: A History of Early Shelburne,** 1982.

Women's Institute of N.S. **History of Port Clyde,** 82 pp., n.d.

VICTORIA COUNTY
County

Patterson, G.G. **History of Victoria County,** 223 pp., 1978.

Local

Lamb, James B. **The Hidden Heritage; Buried Romance at St. Ann's, N.S.** 99 pp., 1975.

MacDonald, D. **Cape North and Vicinity; Pioneer Families . . . ,** 160 pp, 1933.

MacLean, V.J. **The Pioneers of Washabuckt,** 150 pp., 1976.

Rigby, Carle A. **Saint Paul Island, "The Graveyard of the Gulf,"** 36 pp., 1979.

YARMOUTH COUNTY
County

Brown, George S. **Yarmouth, Nova Scotia; A Sequel to Campbell's History,** 524 pp., 1888.

Campbell, John R. **A History of the County of Yarmouth,** 200 pp., 1876.

Lawson, J. Murray, **Yarmouth Past and Present; A Book of Reminiscences,** 647 pp., 1902.

Local

Alexander, David, and Gerry Panting, "The Mercantile Fleet and its Owners: Yarmouth — 1840-1889", **Acadiensis,** VII, 2 (Spring, 1978).

Boucher, Neil. **The Development of an Acadian Village,** 94 pp., 1980.

d'Entremont, Clarence J. **Histoire de Wedgeport,** 91 pp., 1967.

d'Entremont, Henri L. **The Baronnie de Pombcoup and the Acadians,** 192 pp., 1931.

Farish, James C. **Yarmouth, 1821,** 44 pp., 1971.

Gayton, Albert. **Kemptville, Yarmouth County, Nova Scotia: an Historical Sketch,** 19 pp., 1911.

Perry, R.B. **Central Chebogue's Story,** 56 pp., 1970.

Poole E.D. **Annals of Yarmouth and Barrington . . . ,** 133 pp., 1899.

Pothier, Frank J. **Acadians at Home, 1765,** 74 pp., 1957.

Ricker, Jackson. **Historical Sketch of Glenwood and the Argyles, Yarmouth County, Nova Scotia,** 134 pp., 1941.

Surette, Stephen G. **Tusket Wedge,** 92 pp., 1973.

Wedgeport et ses Îles, 108 pp., 1980.

Winter, Kenneth, "The Town of Yarmouth, 1867 and 1923," **NSHR,** I, 1 (1981).

ACADIANS
Arsénault, Bona. **Histoire et généalogie des Acadiens,** 6 vols., 1978.

Daigle, Jean, ed. **The Acadians of the Maritimes: Thematic Studies,** 638 pp., 1982.

d'Entremont, Clarence-J. **Histoire du Cap-Sable de l'an mil au traité de Paris, 1763,** 5 vols., 1981.

Deveau, J. Alponse. **Two Beginnings; a brief Acadian History,** 75 pp., 1980.

Rumilly, Robert. **L'Acadie français (1497-1713),** 254 pp., 1981.

Published Genealogies

The county and community histories will assist both in getting the local background for your family history, and in making you familiar with some of the surnames that are to be found in the particular vicinity. Turning from the geographic approach to that of the more personal, let us now consider family histories that are already in print.

Published genealogies are a very significant resource, not only for the major family which is treated extensively, but frequently too for the light thrown upon the related families. The reliability and thoroughness of such family histories is just as variable as that of the local histories. The prudent reader will not accept every detail as an established fact. It is not a bad idea to take a few points from a published genealogy and check on them by doing your own research. Doing this will help you to gauge the reliability of the particular publication; the more the selected points check out, the more likely that author's reliability in other things. Don't do this just to be critical. In the case of older works you have to recognize that the authors had to rely upon oral tradition for many details in a day when there was no Public

Archives of Nova Scotia and before local historical societies had become as numerous as they are today.

The following listing of family histories is arranged thus: the first column gives the surname of the family traced; the author and publication are shown in the second column. The list is divided to indicate those families having lengthy treatment and those covered in a briefer genealogy. Please note that some were written years previous to publication and that a few have been reprinted.

Some Families Having Printed Genealogies

Adamson — A. Baxter. **The Adamson Family of Dumfrieshire, Scotland and Pictou, N.S.** 13 pp., 1974.

Akin — J.V. Duncanson. **A Listing of the Descendants of Thomas Akin . . . of Falmouth,** 24 pp., 1961.

Allison — Winthrop Bell. **A Genealogical Study,** 292 pp., 1962.

Allison — L.A. Morrison. **The History of the Alison or Allison Family . . . ,** 312 pp., 1893.

Anderson — H. Whidden. **The Anderson Family of Musquodoboit Harbour,** 23 pp., n.d.

Angevine — J.S. Angevine. **The Angevine Family, 1540-1977,** 40 pp., 1977.

Archibald — J.L. Wheeler. **Some of the Archibald Tribe,** 65 pp., 1969.

Armstrong — **Genealogy of the Armstrong Family of Kempt Shore, Hants County . . . ,** 16 pp., 1959.

Avery — S.P. Avery **The Avery, Fairchild, and Park Families,** 151 pp., 1919.

Avery — S.P. Avery. **The Warren, Little, Lothrop, Park, Dix, Whitman, Fairchild, Platt, Wheeler, Lane, and Avery Pedigrees . . . ,** 273 pp., 1925.

Barnhill — C.H. Barnhill. **Barnhill History,** 95 pp., 1979.

Barrett — J.E. Barrett. **The Barretts of Beaverbank, Nova Scotia,** 87 pp., 1980.

Barstow — A.H. Radash, **Barstow Family.**

Bass — C.T. Bass & E.L. Walton. **Descendants of Deacon Samuel Bass and Ann Bass,** 223 pp., 1940.

Beamish — C.T.M. Beamish. **Beamish, A Genealogical Study of A Family in County Cork . . . ,** 275 pp., 1950.

Beckwith — **Marvin Beckwith and his wife Abigail Clark . . . and Their Descendants,** 88 pp., 1899.

Beckwith — P. Beckwith. **The Beckwiths,** 384 pp., 1891.

Beharrell — N.C. Messenger & V.B. Chapman **A Beharrell Family History,** 130 pp., 1974.

Bell — See Allison

Bellefontaine — F.J. Melanson. **Genealogies of . . . Chezzetcook — Bellefontaine,** 143 pp., 1981.

Benjamin — R.A. Benjamin. **Obadiah Benjamin of Nova Scotia,** 16 pp., 1973.

Bent — A.J. Bent. **The Bent Family in America,** 313 pp., 1900.

Bernard — F. Bernard. **De Vendée en Acadie: histoire et généalogie des familles Bernard d' Acadie,** 150 pp., 1972.

Berry — W.W. Walker. **The Berry Family of Clements . . . ,** n.p., 1981.

Bill — J.L. Cobb. **Some Ancestors and Descendants of Edward H. and of Oliver Bill,** 1978.

Bishop — W.R. Boggs & B.R. Bishop. **Genealogy of the Family of Bishops of Horton, Nova Scotia,** 191 pp., 1907.

Black — C. Black. **Historical Record of the Posterity of William Black,** 209 pp., 1885.

Blauveldt — R.B. Blauveldt. **The Blauveldt Family in Nova Scotia . . . ,** 19 pp., n.d.

Blois — Douglas E. Eagles. **The Blois Family of Douglas Township,** 19 pp., 1974.

Boggs — W.E. Boggs. **The Genealogical Record of the Boggs Family,** 95 pp., 1916.

Bonin — F.J. Melanson. **Genealogies of . . . Chezzetcook — Bonin,** 76 pp., 1981.

Bonnevie — F.J. Melanson. **Genealogies of . . . Chezzetcook — Bonnevie,** 132 pp., 1981.

Bourque — Joan Campbell. **Les Descendants d'Antoine Bourg de 1609 à nos jours,** 47 pp., 1978.

Bowser — R.B. Bowser. **A Genealogical Review of the Bowser Family,** 226 pp., 1981.

Brown — E.M. Brown. **Thomas Brown and William Dixson Families,** 12 pp., 1957.

Brownell — G.W. Brownell. **The Brownell Family of New Brunswick and Cumberland County,** 112 pp., 1964.

Buchanan — Maurice G. Buchanan. **Buchanan Ancestry,** 96 pp., 1962.

Buckley — Mary Ella Van Gorden. **Lest We Forget. A Family History concerning Edwin Victor Buckley . . . ,** 1974.

Burgess — B.H. Burgess. **Burgess Genealogy, Kings County, Nova Scotia,** 77 pp., 1941.

Burgess — K.F. Burgess. **Colonists of New England and Nova Scotia; Burgess and Heckman Families,** 134 pp., 1956.

Burnham — D.E. Burnham. **Burnham Genealogy,** 107 pp., 1940.

Burris — M.G. Burris. **My Pioneer Ancestors, an Account of the Burris and Dean Families of Musquodoboit, Nova Scotia,** 293 pp., n.d.

Butler — E.E. Butler. **Butlers and Kinfolk,** 326 pp., 1944.

Caldwell — C.T. Caldwell. **William Coaldwell, Caldwell, or Coldwell of England,** 82 pp., 1910.

Cameron — J.M. Cameron. **The Descendants of Donald Cameron**, 75 pp., 1958.

Campbell — M.E. MacNeil. **Na Caimbeulaich. The Campbells, Descendants of Colin Campbell, Pioneer**, 34 pp., 1970.

Card — T.A. Card. **The Descendants of Richard Card in Kings County, Nova Scotia** 1973.

Carney — D. Carney. **Carney Genealogy**, 373, 160 pp., 1955.

Chesley, — A.E.H. Chesley. **Major Samuel Chesley, J.P., of Upper Granville, Annapolis County, Nova Scotia, and Some of His Descendants and Relatives**, 43 pp., 1952.

Chipman — J.H. Chipman. **A Chipman Genealogy**, 540 pp., 1970.

Churchill — G.A. Churchill. **The Churchill Family in America**, 707 pp., 1904.

Chute — G.M. Chute. **Chute Family in America in the 20th Century**, 123 pp., 1967.

Chute — W.E. Chute. **A Genealogy and History of the Chute Family in America**, 495 pp., 1894.

Cleveland — E.J. Cleveland and H.G. Cleveland. **The Genealogy of the Cleveland and Cleaveland Families**, 3 vols., 1899.

Coates — E.E. Coates. **Descendants of Thomas Coates who came from Yorkshire . . .** , 51 pp., 1978.

Coburn — Heath T. Coburn. **The Bloodstream of an American; Genealogical Gleanings on . . . Francis H. Coburn, Issac Thomas, Bernard Loughery, and Charles F. McEwan**, 60 pp., 1962.

Cochran — A.W.H. Eaton. **The Cochran-Inglis Family of Halifax**, 18 pp., 1899.

Cogswell — E.O. Jameson. **The Cogswells in America.** 683 pp., 1884.

Comeau — E. Comeau. **Généalogie des familles Comeau 1597-1973.** 324 pp., 1973.

Conard — A.L. Luzier. **As The Conard Tree Grows . . .** , 345 pp., 1960.

Copeland — J.M. MacPhee. **A Story of the Copelands from County Wexford . . .** , 66 pp., 1972.

Corkum — A.V. Williams. **The Corkums**, 54 pp., 1975.

Crawford — Hall & Pratt. **Descendants of John & Jane (Goodwin) Crawford of Nova Scotia**, n.p., 1980.

Crozier — R.A. Foulke. **Crozier Family**, 97 pp., 1976.

Cummings — J. Cloud. **Some of the Descendants of Charles Marshall Cummings of Horton, Kings County . . .** , 29 pp., 1980.

Cunnabell — R. Connable. **Pictorial Genealogy of the Cunnabell, Connable . . . Family . . .** , 183 pp., 1886.

Cunningham — L. Cunningham. **The Cunningham Family of Antigonish, N.S.**, 150 pp., 1929.

Cutten — C.B. Cutten. **Genealogy of the Cutten Family of Nova Scotia**, 35 pp., n.d.

Dean — See Burris.

DeBlois — F.B. Fox **Two Huguenot Families,** 120 pp., 1949.

Dechman — R.M. Hattie. **Dechman Family Memoirs,** 93 pp., 1941.

DeLancey — Duncan A. Story. **The DeLanceys, a Romance of a Great Family,** 180 pp., 1931.

Dennis — W.A. Dennis. **The Dennis Genealogy,** 147 pp., 1959.

DeWolf — E.G. & E.M. Salisbury. **Genealogy of the DeWolf Family . . . ,** 60 pp., 1893.

DeWolf — R.L. Weis. **Descendants of the Hon. Benjamin De Wolf . . . of Windsor, N.S.** 16 pp., 1963.

DeWolf — J.E. Wilson. **Genealogy of the DeWolf, Wilson and Young Families,** 18 pp., 1895.

DeWolfe — C.T. Harrington. **A General History of the Harrington, DeWolfe and Tremain Families,** 137 pp., 1938.

Dickenson — N.M. Whiston. **The Loyalist Dickensons of New York,** 27 pp., 1979.

Dickinson — M.S. Dickinson. **Descendants of Captain John and Elizabeth Howland Dickinson of Oyster Bay, Long Island,** 32 pp., n.d.

Dickson — E.F.B. Dewey. **Dickson, Scotch Irish . . . Onslow, Nova Scotia,** 177 pp., 1953.

Dimock — J.D. Marsters. **A Genealogy of the Dimock Family from the Year 1637,** 44 pp., 1899.

Dix — See Avery.

Dixon — J.D. Dixon. **History of Charles Dixon, one of the early English settlers of Sackville, New Brunswick,** 200 pp., 1891.

Dixson — See Brown.

Doane — A.A. Doane. **The Doane Family . . . ,** 2 vols, 1902, 1975, 1976.

Dodge — T.R. Woodward. **Dodge Genealogy; Descendants of Tristram Dodge,** 233 pp., 1904.

Dolliver — L.B. Dolliver. **Dolliver,** 41 pp., 1981.

Dotten — W.L. Dutton. **The Dotten Family in the United States and Canada,** 288 pp., 1970.

Douglas — M.G. Burris. **The Sutherland Family of Six Mile Brook, the Douglas Family of Pictou County, and the Taylor Family of Musquodoboit,** 27 pp., 1937.

Duncanson — J.V. Duncanson. **The Duncanson Family of Horton, Nova Scotia,** 106 pp., 1962.

Eagles — D.E. Eages. **Eagles Families of North America,** 140 pp., 1982.

Eaton — A.W.H. Eaton. **The Eaton Family of Nova Scotia, 1760-1929,** 247 pp., 1929.

Eaton — E.L. Eaton. **The Descendants of Ward Eaton . . .,** 18 pp., 1969.

Embree — J.H. Froggatt. **The Embree Family in Nova Scotia,** 68 pp., 1919.

Estano — **The Family History Book,** n.p., 1981.

Fairbanks — L.S. Fairbanks. **Genealogy of the Fairbanks Family in America, 1633-1897,** 876 pp., 1897.

Fairchild — See Avery.

Fales — D. Fales. **The Fales Family of Bristol, Rhode Island,** 332 pp., 1919.

Fillmore — **An Enquiry on Early Maritime Fillmores,** 41 pp., 1963.

Fillmore — C.L. Fillmore. **The Fillmores of River Philip, Cumberland County,** 28 pp., 1979.

Forbes — C.A. Keating. **Keating and Forbes Families** ... 175 pp., 1920.

Forbes — H.E. Forbes. **Forbes Family of Nova Scotia,** 2nd. ed., 143 pp., 1980.

Frame — D.A. Frame. **Genealogy of the Frame Family,** 27 pp., n.d.

Fraser — **Genealogical Records, Maxwell, Irving, and Fraser Ogg Families of Mount Thom,** 44 pp., n.d.

Fraser — A. MacKenzie. **History of the Frasers of Lovat,** 761 pp., 1896.

Frizzle — E.H. Cameron. **Family of William Frizzle of Inverness County,** N.S. 26 pp., 1967.

Fuller — L. Brainerd. **Genealogy of the Fuller Family,** 43 pp., 1924.

Fullerton — G.W. Fullerton. **The Fullertons of North America,** 92 pp., 1975.

Fulton — **The Fulton Family of Atlantic Canada,** 553 pp., 1979.

Gallant — P. Gallant. **Michel Haché — Gallant et ses descendants,** 2 vols., 1958, 1970.

Gates — C.O. Gates. **Stephen Gates of Hingham and Lancaster, Mass** ..., 370 pp., 1898.

Gayton — A. Gayton. **The Gayton Genealogy** ..., 36 pp., 1918.

Gesner — A.T. Gesner. **The Gesner Family of New York and Nova Scotia,** 30 pp., 1912.

Giffin — F.G. Martin. **Simon Giffin and his Descendants** ..., 238 pp., 1971.

Gillmore — S.F. Tucker. **Partial List of the Descendants of Rev. George Gillmore, A.M., Loyalist of Horton and Windsor, N.S.** 20 pp., 1918.

Girouard — D. Girouard, **L'Album de la famille Girouard.** 51 pp., 1907?

Gouthro — H.M. Carr. **The Four Gouthro Brothers, the Founders of Frenchvale, Cape Breton,** 88 pp., 1976.

Graham — J.M. Graham. **The Graham Family History,** 35 pp., 1929.

Graham — R.H. Graham. **The Story of the New Glasgow Grahams and Allied Families,** 154 pp., 1980.

Grier — J.G. Stevens. **The Descendants of John Grier** ..., 296 pp., 1964.

Grovestone — Powell & Freeman. **A Genealogical Study of the Grovestone Family of Shelburne** ..., 60 pp., 1980.

Hadley — V. Williams. **Genealogy of the Hadley Family.**

Haliburton — R.L. Weis. **Descendants of William Haliburton and Susanna Otis,** 16 pp., 1962.

Halliburton — W.K. Rutherford. **Genealogical History of the Halliburton Family,** 385 pp., 1959.

Harrington — See DeWolfe.

Hart — A. Andrews. **Genealogical History of Deacon Stephen Hart . . . 1632-1875,** 606 pp., 1875.

Hart — J.F. Hart. **History of the Hart Family, Cape Breton Branch,** 40 pp., 1961.

Harvey — M. Harvey. **From Old Scotia to New Scotia, a Family of Harveys . . .** 24 pp., n.d.

Hatfield — A. Hatfield. **Capt. John Hatfield, Loyalist,** 103 pp., 1943.

Hattie — R.M. Hattie & J.H. Kirk. **Hattie Family Memoirs,** 261 pp., 1936.

Healy — C.W. Carrier. **Healy History,** 101 pp., 1963.

Hebb — G.P. Hebb, **The Early Life and History of the Hebb Family, 1978.**

Heckman — See Burgess

Higgins - J. Reid. **A History of the Higgins Family of Higginsville, Halifax County,** 47 pp., 1978.

Hingley — A.E. Marble. **The History and Genealogy of the Hingley Family in N.S.,** 233 pp., 1966.

Hoar(e) — D.W. Hoare. **Digest of Ancestry . . . of the Hoar(e) Family . . . ,** 113 pp., 1975.

Houghton — **History and Genealogy of the Houghton Family,** 100 pp., 1896.

Hoyt — R.W. Wiles. **Genealogy of the Hoyt and Wiles Families,** 47 pp., 1955.

Hulbert — J.M. Cameron. **American Pioneers in Antigonish.**

Hunter — M.S. Smiley & I.S. Young. **History of the Hunter Family, 1769-1960,** 255 pp., 1960.

Illsley — C.E. Illsley. **The Illsley Genealogy,** 56 pp., 1964.

Inglis — See Cochran.

Ingraham — A.W. Thompson. **The Name and Family of Ingraham,** 47 pp., 1959.

Irish — W.L. & S.B. Irish. **Descendants of John Irish, the Immigrant . . . ,** 662 pp., 1964.

Irish — H.H. Olding. **Irish and Allied Families,** 53 pp., n.d.

Irving — See Fraser.

Jackson — E.E. Jackson. **Cape Breton and the Jackson Kith and Kin,** 264 pp., 1971.

Jefferson — C.Q. Jefferson. **Genealogical Listings of the Jefferson Family . . . ,** 84 pp., 1975.

Jess — M.M. Payzant. **The Payzant and Allied Jess and Juhan Families . . . ,** 452 pp., 1970.

Johnson — G.A. Johnson. **History and Genealogy of the Acadian Johnsons,** 323 pp., 1980.

Johnstone — C.B. Johnstone. **The Annandale Johnstones, Ancient and Modern,** 33 pp., 1935.

Juhan — See Jess.

Julien — F.J. Melanson. **Genealogies of . . . Chezzetcook — Julien,** 49 pp., 1981.

Kaulbach — R.E. Kaulbach. **The Genealogy of the Kaulbach Family of Lunenburg County,** 24 pp., 1960.

Keating — See Forbes.

Kent — O.M. Kent. **Family Tree of James Kent,** 15 pp., 1967.

Kinsman — D.M. Kinsman. **The Genealogy of the Family of Joseph Alexander Kinsman . . .,** 66 pp., 1974.

Knowles — V.K. Hufbauer. **Descendants of Richard Knowles, 1637-1973,** 852 pp., 1974.

Lane — See Avery.

Langille — G. Byers. **The North Shore Langilles of Nova Scotia,** 23 pp., 1977.

Lapierre — F.J. Melanson. **Genealogies of . . . Chezzetcook — Lapierre,** 148 pp., 1981.

Little — See Avery.

Locke — A.H. Locke. **A History and Genealogy of Capt. John Locke, 1627-1696 . . .,** 720 pp., 1973.

Logan — E. Bryson. **The Logan Family, 1816-1976,** 14 pp., 1976.

Logan — G. Logan. **The Logan Grantees of Truro, N.S.,** 149 pp., 1967.

Logan — H.A. Logan. **The Logans of Amherst,** 98 pp., 1967.

Logan — O. Logan. **One Family of Logans in N.S.,** 1966.

Longley — R.D. Longley. **Longley Family,** 39 pp., 1952.

Lord — K. Lord. **Genealogy of the Descendants of Thomas Lord,** 482 pp., 1946.

Lothrop — See Avery.

Loughery — See Coburn.

MacAulay — D.M. MacKenzie. **The MacAulay Family of Lewis,** 40 pp., n.d.

McCurdy — H.P. Blanchard. **Genealogical Record . . . of the McCurdys of Nova Scotia,** 228 pp., 1930.

Macdonald — H.N. MacDonald. **Macdonald and Mackinnon Families,** 31 pp., 1937.

MacDonald — J.S. McGivern. **Truly Canadian, the MacDonalds of Red Bank and Broad Cove,** 113 pp., 1968.

McDuffie — E.D. MacPhee. **The Mythology, Traditions and History of . . . MacDuffie Clan,** 5 vols, 1972.

McEwan — See Coburn.

McGillivray - John Doull. **Reverend Alexander McGillivray. D.D.,** 24 pp., 1938.

MacIntosh — W.R. MacIntosh. **A Record of the Descendants of Robert and Anne MacIntosh,** 18 pp., 1955.

MacIvor — J.M. MacIvor. **The MacIvor Clan in Canada,** 53 pp., ca. 1922.

McKay — W.L. Kean. **The Genealogy of Hugh McKay and his Lineal Descendants . . .,** 76 pp., 1895.

MacKenzie — T.G. MacKenzie. **The MacKenzies of River John,** 36 pp., n.d.

McKinnon — See Macdonald.

MacLean — A.K. MacLean — **A Brief Historic Account of Angus ... Mac-Lean ... of Glen Bard and Ohio,** 84 pp., 1963.

McNutt — T.H. Lodge. **The McNutt Family,** 35 pp., 1957.

MacPherson — L.C. MacPherson. **A History of a MacPherson Family from Pictou ... ,** 35 pp., 1960.

McRae — E.M. MacLeod. **Geonealogy of Christopher and Mary McRae of Cape Breton,** 52 pp., 1980.

Manette — F.J. Melanson. **Genealogies of ... Chezzetcook — Manet,** 59 pp., 1981.

Maxwell — See Fraser.

Mayer — B. Mayer. **Memoir and Genealogy of the Maryland and Pennsylvania Family of Mayer,** 179 pp., 1878.

Mayet — F.J. Melanson. **Genealogies of ... Chezzetcook — Mayet,** 52 pp., 1981.

Melvin — E.W. Leavitt. **Palmer Groups. John Melvin of Charlestown and Concord, Mass., and his Descendants,** 450 pp., 1901-1905.

Miller — W.A. Dennis. **The Miller Descendants ... ,** 23 pp., 1961.

Miller — W.B. Tucker. **The Romance of the Palatine Millers,** 369 pp., 1929.

Miner — T.M. Johnson. **The Miner Family, Horton Branch** 96 pp., 1929.

Morehouse — I.M.S. Morehouse. **330 Years of Morehouse Genealogy, 1640-1970.** 542 pp., 1978.

Morrow — S. Stairs. **Stairs, Morrow Family History,** 264 pp., 1906.

Morse — D.S. & A.S. Morse. **A Preliminary Genealogy of the Annapolis Morses ... ,** 61 pp., 1977.

Mosher — W. Mosher. **Chronological History of the Mosher Family ... ,** 66 pp., 1891.

Murphy — F.J. Melanson. **Genealogies of ... Chezzetcook — Murphy,** n.p., 1981.

Murray — W.M. Goodwin. **The "Inchure" Murrays of Nova Scotia,** 15 pp., c. 1977.

Mutch — J.R. Mutch. **Genealogy of the Mutch Family,** 94 pp., 1929.

Nelson — E.E. Coates. **Descendants of Peter Nelson ... of Leamington, Cumberland Co.,** 28 pp., 1978.

Newcomb — B.M. Newcomb. **Andrew Newcomb, 1618-1686, and his Descendants,** 1021 pp., 1923.

Nickerson — **The Nickerson Family ... ,** 3 vols., 1973-1976.

Olding — H.H. Olding, Jr. **Olding and Allied Families,** 107 pp., 1977.

Outhouse — L. Cunningham. **The Outhouse Family of Tiverton, Nova Scotia,** 87 pp., 1938.

Page — L.M. Case & P. Sanderson. **The Family of John Page of Haverhill, Mass ... ,** 251 pp., 1977.

Park — See Avery.

Parker — W.F. Parker. **Daniel McNeill Parker, M.D., His Ancestry ...**, 604 pp., 1910.

Patterson — D.F. Patterson. **The Pattersons of Kings County, Nova Scotia,** 182 pp., 1977.

Payzant — J.V. Duncanson. **Descendants of Louis Paisant or Payzant (1698-1756),** 27 pp., 1961.

Payzant — See Jess.

Pearson — E.L. Pearson. **A Pearson Family History,** 57 pp., 1962.

Perkins — G.A. Perkins. **The Family of John Perkins of Ipswich, Mass.,** 3 vols., 1884-1889.

Petitpas — F.J. Melanson. **Genealogies of ... Chezzetcook — Petitpas,** 108 pp., 1981.

Platt — See Avery.

Porter — I.R. Porter. **The Porter Genealogy ...,** 20 pp., n.d.

Potter — J.S. Potter. **History and Genealogy of the late Rev. Israel Potter's Branch of the Potter Family,** 21 pp., 1885.

Prescott — William Prescott. **The Prescott Memorial ...,** 653 pp., 1870.

Purdy — C.C. Purdy. **Gabriel Purdy, His Ancestors & Descendants,** ? pp., 1983.

Pushee — J.M. Cameron. **American Pioneers in Antigonish,** 48 pp., 1982.

Rafuse — A. Mahon. **The Family Rafuse 460 years,** 86 pp., 1982.

Raymond — Samuel Raymond. **Genealogies of the Raymond Families of New England ...,** 298 pp., 1886.

Redden — M.S. Smiley. **History of the Redden Family ...,** 1795-1965, 213 pp., 1965.

Reynolds — H.C. Reynolds. **Genealogical and Historical Sketch of My Family, 1774-1972,** 29 pp., 1972.

Richan — S.H. Richan. **The Book of Richan,** 39 pp., 1936.

Ringer — R.L. Ringer. **The Ringer Family of Nova Scotia ...,** 47 pp., n.d.

Robichaud — D. Robichaud. **Les Robichaud: histoire et généalogie,** 264 pp., 1968.

Roma — F.J. Melanson. **Genealogies of ... Chezzetcook — Roma,** 132 pp., 1981.

Ross — Harry R. Brown & B. Ross. **The Rosses of Rossville ...,** 1978.

Samson — **Echos du Tricentenaire des familles Samson en Amérique,** 40 pp., 1973.

Sanford — J.M. Sanford. **President John Sanford of Boston ..., 1605-1965,** 487 pp., 1969.

Sargent — H.L. Doane. **The Barrington Sargents,** 38 pp., 1916.

Sargent — E.W. Sargent. **Epes Sargent of Gloucester and his Descendants,** 323 pp., 1923.

Savary — A.W. Savary. **A Genealogical and Biographical Record of the Savary Families,** 266 pp., 1893.

Savoie — C. Hamelin. **La Généalogie de le famille Savoie . . .** , 64 pp., 1912.

Schurman — Ross G. Graves. **William Schurman, Loyalist . . . and his Descendants,** 2 vols, 1973.

Seely — W.P. Bacon. **Ancestry of Daniel James Seely and Charlotte Louisa Vail,** 185 pp., n.d.

Shannon — G.E. Hodgen. **Shannon Genealogy,** 578 pp., 1905.

Shaw — R.H. Shaw. **Shaw Family in Nova Scotia.** 57 pp., 1962.

Shaw — D. Turner. **Genealogy of the Descendants of John Shaw and Mary (Burness),** 548 pp., 1973.

Sibley — J. Wright. **The Sibleys of Wittenberg, N.S.,** 35 pp., 1946.

Simmonds — F.W. Simmonds. **John and Susan and Some of their Descendants . . . ,** 222 pp., 1940.

Sinclaire — S.L. Daub. **The Sinclaire Family of Belfast . . . ,** 91 pp., 1965.

Smiley — **History of the Smiley Families, 1828-1960,** 93 pp., n.d.

Smith — R.H. Freeman. **My Branch of the Descendants of Ralph Smith,** 33 pp., 1975.

Smith — N. Smith. **History of the Smith Family,** 200 pp., 1862.

Smith — F.W. Smith. **History of Port Hood . . . with the Genealogy of the Smith Family,** 275 pp., 1967.

Snow — S. Carey. **Captain Jabez Snow and some of his Descendants,** 30 pp., 1979.

Speidel — S.M. Spidell. **The Speidel Family of Lunenburg County,** rev. ed., 99 pp., 1977.

Spurr — E.D. Fincher. **Spurr Genealogy,** 108 pp., 1966.

Stairs — H.G. Stairs. **Stairs of Halifax,** 173 pp., 1962.

Stairs — See Morrow.

Staples — **The Staples Family of Staples Brook, Colchester County,** 35 pp., 1980.

Steeves — Esther C. Wright. **Samphire Greens, a Story of the Steeves . . . ,** 94 pp., 1961.

Steeves — Esther C. Wright. **The Steeves Descendants,** 921 pp., 1966.

Stevens — R.K. & Cj. Stevens. **The Stevens Families of Nova Scotia,** 450 pp., 1979.

Stewart — E.S. Hill. **A Sense of Continuity, the Stewarts of Douro,** 98 pp., n.d.

Sutherland — See Douglas.

Tattrie — G.M. Haliburton. **The Tattrie Family of River John, 1752-1952,** 20 pp., 1953.

Taylor — See Douglas.

Taylor — J.W. & E.M. Taylor. **Montross; a Family History,** 861 pp., 1958.

Terry — S. Terry. **Notes of Terry Families** . . . , 343 pp., 1887.

Thomas — See Coburn.

Tingley — M.M. Frye. **The Tingley Book Revised,** 4 vols., 1970-1977.

Trask — G.G. Trask. **Elias Trask, his children and their succeeding race,** 205 pp., 1979.

Tremain — See DeWolf.

Troop — J.E.D. Troop. **Fragmentary History of the Family Troop, Troup, Throop(e),** 160 pp., 1976.

Truman — Howard Truman. **The Chignecto Isthmus and its First Settlers,** 278 pp., 1902.

Tufts — J.F. Tufts. **Tufts Family History** . . . , 280 pp., c. 1963.

Tupper — E. Tupper. **Tupper Genealogy, 1578-1971,** 919 pp., 1972.

Turnbull — J.F. Turnbull. **History and Genealogy of the Turnbull Family of Digby, N.S.,** 18 pp., 1960.

Vaughan — H.S. Vaughan. **History and Genealogy of the Vaughan Family,** 90 pp., 1969.

Verge — G.B. Kinsman. **Verge: a family history of two brothers,** 43 pp., 1980.

Warren — See Avery.

Waterman — D.L. Jacobus. **The Waterman Family,** 2 vols., 1939, 1942.

Waters — M. Waters. **Waters in Depth,** 1978.

Weldon — W.S. Weldon. **The Family of Weldon in Canada, 1732-1952,** 126 pp., 1953.

Wentworth — C.H. Johnson. **Families of Wentworth,** 21 pp., n.d.

West — Terrence M. Punch. **The Wests of Halifax and Lunenburg,** 18 pp., 1976.

West — M.A. Ells. **West Lines,** 112 pp., 1978.

Wheeler — See Avery.

Whidden — D.G. Whidden. **Genealogical Record of the Antigonish Whiddens,** 24 pp., 1930.

Whidden — H.H. Whidden & P.W. Barlow. **The Whidden Family of Nova Scotia,** 173 pp., 1980.

White — Mary Archibald. **Gideon White, Loyalist,** 64 pp., 1975.

White — A.L. White. **Genealogy of the Descendants of John White** . . . , 2 vols., 1900.

Whitman — See Avery.

Whitman — C.H. Farnham. **History of the Descendants of John Whitman,** 1246 pp., 1889.

Whitman — C.B. Whitman. **The Annapolis Valley Whitmans,** 246 pp., 1972.

Whitney — S.W. Phoenix. **The Whitney Family of Connecticut** . . . , 3 vols. 1878.

Wickwire — A.M. Wickwire. **Genealogy of the Wickwire Family,** 283 pp., 1909.

Wiles — See Hoyt.

Williams — J.M. Cameron. **American Pioneers in Antigonish,** 48 pp., 1982.

Wilson — See DeWolf.

Wood — H.B. Howe. **Yorkshire to Westchester, a Chronicle of the Wood Family,** 290 pp., 1948.

Woodworth — M.E. Woodworth. **Descendants of Stephen Woodworth, 1769-1850,** 13 pp., 1966.

Worden — E.S. Worden. **Some Information about the Name Worden . . . ,** 26 pp., 1961.

Young — See DeWolf.

Smaller Genealogies

All the foregoing references appear in a book about one or a few families. Each of those publications was a dozen pages or longer, and is available in one or more of the libraries of Nova Scotia. The group which follows next is composed of smaller genealogies found among the holdings of the Public Archives of Nova Scotia. There are 44 references in this section, arranged as was the preceding listing.

Allen — C.S. Stayner, "The Allen Family of Dartmouth, N.S.", MS in P.A.N.S., 1950.

Archibald — E. Archibald, "Chart of the Archibald Family, 1693-1974," 1974.

Bayer — C.S. Stayner, "Bayer Family of Halifax and Rockingham," MS in P.A.N.S., 1950.

Bayne — E.B. Spice, "Bayne Family, Scotland, Pictou, and Halifax . . . ," 1976.

Beaton — D.P. Johnson, "The History of the MacDonalds, Johnsons, and Beatons," MS in P.A.N.S., 1973.

Belliveau — "Genealogy of the Belliveau Family in N.S., 1631-1966," 1973.

Benson — "The Christopher Benson Genealogy," 1957.

Beveridge — "The Beveridge Family," 1909.

Boutilier — "Genealogy of the Boutilier Family," c. 1966.

Burgess — "Burgess Family," MS in P.A.N.S., 1979.

Crockett — E.A. Crockett, "The Joseph R. Crockett Family," 1978.

Crowe — M.S. Cleveland, "Crowe Family History, 1700-1972," 1972.

Dartt — Mrs. Walter Wulff, "Charts of the Dartt Family, 1750-1964," 1977.

D'Entremont — "Ancestral Chart of Joseph D'Entremont, West Pubnico," Chart in P.A.N.S.

Embree — E.P. Embree, "Descendants of Col. Samuel Embree . . . ," 1917.

Etter — C.S. Stayner, "Genealogy of the Etter Family of Chester . . . ," MS in P.A.N.S., 1953.

Frost — A.A. Doane, "The Frost Genealogy," 1910.

Godfrey — J.M. Godfrey, "Sketch of the Godfrey Family of Halifax," 1922.

Gordon — Ross G. Graves, "The Gordon Family of Hants County ...," 1951.

Goudge — C.S. Stayner, "Goudge Family of Halifax and Windsor," MS in P.A.N.S., 1950.

Harding — Harris — G.S. Brown, "The Harding and Harris Families," 1913.

Hemeon — G.S. Brown, "The Hemeon Family," 1909.

Hind — J.V. Duncanson, "A Listing of the Descendants of Henry Yould Hind," 1961.

Hirtle — A.G.G. & J. Hirtle, "The Hirtles in Canada," microfilm in P.A.N.S.

Irwin — "The Irwin Genealogy," MS in P.A.N.S.

Johnson — See Beaton

Keddy — C.S. Stayner, "The Kedy or Keddy Family of Nova Scotia," MS in P.A.N.S., 1954.

Kenney — A.A. Doane, "The Kenney Genealogy," 1909.

Kenty — H.J. Kenty, "Genealogical Record of the Kenty Family in Nova Scotia," c. 1970.

Kinnie — J.V. Duncanson, "A Listing of the Descendants of Nathan Kinnie ...," 1962.

Lowe — A.C. Lowe, "The Family of John Smith Lowe and Miriam Lockhart," 1967.

MacDonald — See Beaton.

MacKenzie — A.M. Sinclair, "The Mackenzies of Applecross, Scotland," 1901.

McLellan — John Doull, "The McLellans of McLellans Brook," 1961.

Marshall — B. Marshall, "The Marshall Family of Pictou County, Nova Scotia," n.d.

Oakes — "Oakes Family History," 1972.

Payzant — C.S. Stayner, "The Payzant Family of Nova Scotia," manuscript in P.A.N.S., 1952.

Pinckney — C.S. Brown, "The Pinckney Family," 1909.

Potter — L.W. Potter, "Descendants of David Henry and Elizabeth (Bacon) Potter," 1969.

Rhuland — E.T. Bliss, "Rhuland, Pioneer Settler in Lunenburg," 1964.

Rust — G.S. Brown, "The Rust Family," 1909.

Stewart — G.S. Stayner, "The Stewart Family of Halifax and Amherst, N.S.," MS in P.A.N.S., 1954.

Theakston — "The Theakston Family," n.d.

Winter(s) — C.A. Winters, "New World Adventures; a History of Philip Winter and his Descendants," 1950.

Published Articles

This group of genealogies is made up of those which have appeared in articles published in one of the following eleven magazines: **Acad.** = **Acadiensis**, old series; **IA** = **The Irish Ancestor; IG** = **The Irish Genealogist; JCHAS** = **Journal** of the Cork Historical and Archaeological Society; **NEHGR** = **New England Historical and Genealogical Register; FCAGR** = **French Canadian and Acadian Genealogical Review; NSHQ** = **Nova Scotia Historical Quarterly; NSHR** = **Nova Scotia Historical Review; NSHS** = **Collections** of Nova Scotia Historical Society; **SHA** = **Cahiers** de la Société Historique Acadienne. **SGCF** = **Memoires de le Société Généalogique Canadienne-française; RCA** = **Report Concerning Canadian Archives for the Year.** The same format is followed as before.

Affleck — See Thompson.
Ast — T.M. Punch, "Irish Miscellany; some have gone from us," **NSHQ**, X, 1, 1980.
Ast — T.M. Punch, "Irish Miscellany; some have gone from us," **NSHQ**, X, 1, 1980.
Babineau — G. Bineau, "Nicolas Babineau ancêtre de tous les Babineau et Bineau de l'Amérique," **SGCF**, XVIII, 1967.
Bachman — F.A. Bauckman, "John Baptist Bachman of Lunenburg . . . ," **NSHQ**, V, 3, 1975.
Banks — C.E. Banks, "The Bank(e)s Family of Maine," **NEHGR**, XLIV, 1890
Banks — J. Furber Marshall, "A Banks Family of Nova Scotia," **NSHQ**, VII, 2, 1977.
Beamish — T.M. Punch, "Beamish of Kilvurra and Halifax," **NSHQ**, IX, 3, 1979.
Belcher — W.H. Whitmore, "Notes on the Belcher Family," **NEHGR**, XXVII, 1873.
Belliveau — P. Gaudet, "Famille Belliveau," **RAC**, II, 1, (1906).
Blackadar — C.St.C. Stayner, "The Blackadar Family of Halifax," **NSHR**, I, 1, 1981.
Boudreau — "Aucoin de Chéticamp, Boudreau de Chéticamp," **SHA**, IV, 1972.
Bourgeois — P. Gaudet, "Famille Bourgeois," **RAC**, II, A, III, (1906).
Breau — A Godbout "Origine des Brau Acadiens," **SGCF**, IX, 1958.
Burns — A.E. Marble, "The Burns Family of Wilmot Township . . . ," **NSHQ**, VIII, 2, 1978.
Byles — A.W.H. Eaton, "The Byles Family," **NEHGR**, LXIX, 1915.
Cassidy — T.M. Punch, "Irish Miscellany . . . ," **NSHQ**, X, 1, 1980.
Chipman — H. Chipman, "A Chipman Family History," **NEHGR**, LXXXI, 1927.
Colford — T.M. Punch, "Irish Miscellany . . . ," **NSHQ**, X, 1, 1980.

Cormier — A Godbout, "Origines des Cormier," **SGCF,** IV, 1951.

Cotter — T.M. Punch, "Irish Miscellany . . . ," **NSHQ,** X, 1, 1980.

Creamer — T.M. Punch, "Irish Miscellany . . . ," **NSHQ,** X, 1, 1980.

DeBlois — A.W.H. Eaton, "Old Boston Families, the DeBlois Family," **NEHGR,** LXVII, 1913.

Doucet — Mme Doucet, "Généalogie des familles Doucet Souche Acadienne," **SGCF,** VI, 1955.

Fairweather — G. Haliburton, "Genealogy of the descendants of David Fairweather of West River and River John," **NSHQ,** IX, 4, 1979.

Fellows — L.B. Cousins, "The Fellows Family of Granville, N.S.," **NSHQ,** VIII, 1, 1978.

Fenwick — G.C. Fenwick, "The Fenwick Family in Nova Scotia," **NSHS,** XVII, 1913.

Finucane — George F. Mott, "Finucane of County Clare," **IA,** I, 1, 1969.

Fultz — L.Y. Kernaghan & T.M. Punch, "The Fultz Family of Sackville, Halifax County . . . ," **NSHR,** II, 1, 1982.

Gerrish — A.W.H. Eaton, "The Gerrish Family (Family of Capt. John Gerrish)," **NEHGR,** LXVII, 1913.

Gorham — F.W. Sprague, "Jabez Gorham of Plymouth, Mass . . . ," **NEHGR,** LIX, 1905.

Haliburton — A.W.H. Eaton, "The Haliburton Family . . . ," **NEHGR,** LXXI, 1917.

Harris — R.F. Harris, "A Pioneer Harris Family . . . of Pictou," **NSHS,** XXXIII, 1961.

Harvie — R.P. Harvey, "John Harvie . . . of Newport, Nova Scotia," **NSHQ,** VI, 4, 1976.

Henry — Phyllis R. Blakeley, "William Alexander Henry," **NSHS,** XXXVI, 1967.

Howe — T.M. Punch & A.E. Marble, "The Family of John Howe, Halifax . . . ," **NSHQ,** VI, 3, 1976.

Inglis — A.W.H. Eaton, "Bishop Charles Inglis and His Decendants," **Acad.,** VIII, 1908.

Landry — P. Gallant, "Premières familles de Landry en Acadie," **SHA,** IV, 1973, 1974.

Langille — Gerald Byers, "The North Shore Langilles of Nova Scotia," **NSHQ,** VII, 3, 1977.

LaVache — S.A. White, "The LaVache Family of Arichat, Cape Breton," **NSHQ,** VII, 1, 1977.

LeBlanc — S.A. White, "Coste and leBlanc Families," **FCAGR,** III, 1971.

Léger — L. Campeau, "La famille Léger," **SGCR,** V, 1953.

McCabe — A.E. Marble, "James McCabe Genealogy; a pre-'Hector' Settler in Pictou County," **NSHQ,** V, 4, 1975.

McKay — McPherson — M. Robinson, "The McKays and McPhersons," **NSHS,** XXXVII, 1970.

MacKay, McLennan — J.G. Gibson, "Piper John MacKay and Roderick McLennan: a Tale of Two Immigrants and their incomplete Genealogy," **NSHR,** II, 2 (1982).

MacQuarrie — E.F. Perry & M. Kegley, "Descendants of John Lauchlin MacQuarrie of Caledonia," **Clan MacQuarrie of Atlantic Canada Newsletter,** II, 1, June 1982.

Maxner — J.V. Duncanson, "The Maxners of Lunenburg and Windsor," **NSHQ,** X, 2, 1980.

Melanson — R.J. Auger, "Melanson Genealogy," **FCAGR,** II, 1969.

Morris — E. Crathorne, "The Morris Family, Surveyors-General," **NSHQ,** VI, 2, 1976.

Newton — A.W.H. Eaton, "Hon. Hibbert Newton . . . ," **NEHGR,** LXVIII, 1914.

Prescott — T.M. Punch, "Jonathan Prescott, M.D. Vincit Qui Patitur," **NSHQ,** IX, 1, 1979.

Punch — T.M. Punch, "The Punch Family," **IG,** III, 6, 1961.

Punch — T.M. Punch, "Pons to Punch," **IA,** II, 1, 1970.

Rawley — T.M. Punch, "An Irish Miscellany . . . ," **NSHQ,** X, 1, 1980.

Raymond — Ann Raymond, "Daniel Raymond of Yarmouth — a Pre-Loyalist Settler in Western Nova Scotia," **NSHQ,** VIII, 3, 4, 1978.

Ritchie — M.C. Ritchie, "The Beginnings of a Canadian Family," **NSHS,** XXIV, 1938.

Rogers — A.B. Robertson, "The Family of Rolen Rogers . . . King's County," **NSHQ,** IX, 2, 1979.

Surette — Neil Boucher, "The Surettes of Eel Brook . . . ," **NSHQ,** IX, 1, 1979.

Tattrie — G. Haliburton, "A Tattrie Line of Descent," **NSHR,** I, 2, 1981.

Thompson — A.E. Marble & T.M. Punch, "Sir J.S.D. Thompson: A Prime Minister's Family Connections," **NSHQ,** VII, 4, 1977.

Tobin — T.M. Punch, "Tobin Genealogy," **NSHQ,** V, 1, 1975.

Trahan — G. Massignon, "Les Trahan d'Acadie," **SHA,** I 5, 1964.

Uniacke — R. FitzGerald — Uniacke, "Some Old County Cork Families, I. The Uniackes of Youghal," **JCHAS,** III, old series, 1894.

Weatherhead — R.C. Graves, "The Weatherhead Family of Upper Rawdon," **NSHQ,** V, 2, 1975.

West — T.M. Punch, "The Wests of Halifax and Lunenburg," **NSHQ,** VI, 1, 1976.

Wightman — G.B. Manzer, "The Wightman Family," **Acad.,** VII, 1907.

In sum, we have here a list of 405 books, pamphlets and articles that contain some information about a family which has lived in Nova Scotia. Allowing for the fact that a few surnames have been treated more than once, there remains a total of 356 family names about which there is something in print. When you consider the number of local and county histories which contain genealogical material, you will realize that there has been much work done in and about our families. You will also appreciate that far more remains to be done. However, if you are interested in a family whose name has been listed, you would be wise to look at the item. It could save you a lot of time and money. Do not understand me to recommend any or all of the above publications. I mention them for what they are. There is a great variation in quality of these works, and it would be invidious to separate them accordingly.

As a purely personal prejudice, I tend to regard work done by someone not of the studied family to be more likely to be objective, but also more apt to be impersonal, whereas the enthusiast writing his own lineage will often wax eloquent and informative in his account of the family, but may stretch out or omit the facts upon which his tale is based. Some, such as W.E. Chute, managed well the fine art of offering "inside" information without the sacrifice of objectivity or of accuracy. Others were not so fortunate. Another way to consider these books is by their dates of publication. Newer work is usually more to our contemporary taste than are the older and often antiquarian efforts. Several of the early authors loved to launch into stirring tales of derring-do, tragic occasions and melancholy woes, but, again, some of the moderns can be justly blamed for writing minimal histories. The names and dates are well researched and are probably as accurate as ever they will be, but names and dates do not evoke personalities or the times through which they lived. The choice of what you will do is largely yours, but I hope you will combine accuracy with some human interest in your finished family history.

Local Historians

Over the years, local genealogists have performed very useful work on the families living within their areas of specialization. Much of their material in the form of notes has been deposited in libraries and in the Public Archives of Nova Scotia. To help researchers looking for certain family names, and to illustrate the wealth that these sources contain, here is an example. At the Archives you will find M.G.9, No. 109, "Crowell's Scrapbook of New Englanders in Nova Scotia." These articles were published between 1927 and 1935 in the **Yarmouth Herald** and the **Yarmouth Telegram.** Therefore, it is in a way a published secondary source. The scrapbook at the reading room of the Archives contains genealogical data about the following 313 families. In a few cases, more than one family of a surname is included in the collection. The families are:

Agard	Bancroft	Babcock	Beckwith	Bliss	Brattle
Allen	Banks	Baker	Belcher	Blowers	Breck
Atkins	Barnard	Balcom	Berry	Boomer	Brenton
Atwood	Barnes	Bawsett	Binney	Boutineau	Brewster
Auchmuty	Bartlett	Beaman	Blair	Bradford	Brinley
Avery	Bass	Bearse	Blanchard	Bradshaw	Broughton

48

Bunker
Burbank
Butler
Byles
Cahoon
Caldwell
Chandler
Chase
Chesley
Chipman
Church
Churchill
Chadsey
Chamberlain
Champion
Clark
Cleveland
Cobb
Coffin
Coggin
Coleman
Collins
Cook
Cooke
Corning
Cossett
Covell
Crandall
Crocker
Crosby
Cross
Crowell
Cunnabell
Cunningham
Cushing
Cushman
Cutler
Dakin
Davis
Deane
DeBlois
De(e)ring
Delap
Dexter
Dimock
Doane
Doggett
Do(ugh)ty
Douglas
Dudley
Durfee
Eddy
Eldridge

Ellenwood
Ellis
Elwell
Fales
Farnsworth
Fellows
Fillis
Fisher
Folger
Foote
Foster
Foye
Freeman
Frost
Gallup
Gannet
Gardner
Gay
Gilbert
Gillmore
Goodwin
Gore
Gorham
Gould
Gowan
Gray
Green
Haliburton
Hall
Hamilton
Harding
Hardwick
Harlow
Haskell
Hersey
Hibbard
Hicks
Higgins
Hilton
Hoar
Holmes
Homer
Hooper
Hopkins
Horswell
Houghton
Hovey
Howe
Hunt
Huntington
Hurd/Heard
Hutchinson
Ingersoll

Irwin
Jennison
Johannot
Jones
Kempton
Kendrick
Kennedy
Kent
Killam
Kimball
King
Kinsman
Kirby
Knowles
Ladd
Larkin
Laskie
Lawson
Leadbetter
Lee
Leonard
Lewis
Lillis
Lincoln
Locke
Lockwood
Longfellow
Longley
Lord
Lovett
Lyde
McGray
McKean/McKeen
McNutt
Macy
Mascarene
Mason
Mayhew
Mayo
Melvin
Merriam
Merrick
Miller
Minns
Minot
Mitchell
Moore
Moorhead
Morgan
Mor(r)ison
Morris
Morton
Mosher

Moulton
Mumford
Murray
Newell
Newton
Nickerson
Noble
Nutting
Oliver
Osborne
Paine
Parish
Partridge
Patch
Patten
Pearson
Pease
Pepperell
Perkins
Perry
Peters
Phelps
Pierce
Pierson
Pingree
Pinkham
Pitts
Poole
Porter
Prescott
Prince
Purdy
Putnam
Rand
Randall
Rathbone
Redding
Reynolds
Rice
Ring
Robbins
Robertson
Robie
Rogers
Ruggles
Russell
Sabin
Sabine
Salter
Sanderson
Sandford
Sargent
Scott

Seabury
Sears
Seccomb
Sewell
Shannon
Shaw
Shurtleff
Smith
Snow
Sollows
Southack
Stanwood
Steadman
Stearns
Stuart
Sumner
Swain
Symonds
Tailer
Tarbell
Temple
Terry
Thomas
Thompson
Thorndike
Thorp
Tinkham
Townshend
Tracy
Trask
Trefry
Tucker
Turner
Tyng
Upham
Vetch
Viets
Vincent
Waldo
Walker
Walter
Waterman
Watmough
Weare
Webster
Weeks
Welton
Wentworth
Weston
Wheelock
Whipple
White
Whitman

49

Wilson	Witter	Woodbury	Woodworth	Wyman
Winslow	Wood	Woodward	Worth	Yuill
Witham				

The Newspaper

A major source of assistance for those who find that they have a "missing period" from the church and community records is the newspaper. Many of the township books had passed their prime by 1820, and many church records had either not yet begun or have been lost for those early years. Newspaper coverage of vital events is, of course, much more important when the other types of records are inaccesible or non-existent.

Early newspapers — in Nova Scotia, this means from 1752 to 1867 — did not report everything. Some of them at times did their seeming best to report nothing. The local news in a small community did not require publication to obtain currency. A town of less than twelve thousand people had no need for five columns of obituaries, and the editors did not attempt to change that for many years.

Newspapers were selective in their coverage of vital events. Virtually no births were reported, unless they were in the family of a very high personage and his lady, or unless the birth was clearly unusual — of the "lady has quadruplets in a row boat" variety. The areas in more regular communication with a newspaper (e.g., Halifax, Pictou, Liverpool, Yarmouth) received noticeably more ink than did the outports.

Ethnic origin and religion played at least some part in whether or not your death or marriage received the dignity of newspaper attention. Acadians and Indians failed to get a fair shake, while Irish Catholics and Scots Highlanders did little better. This situation was due, not to ethnic or sectarian prejudice, but to geographic remoteness of many of the districts where such groups lived. Families of American, English and Lunenburg backgrounds did enjoy the "lion's share" of the reporting. The Irish and Scots, being relative newcomers, were also less likely to be known generally in the community and colony, and the death of one more "Paddy Murphy" or "Hughie MacKay" was not regarded as newsworthy. The treatment of black people by the early press was not praiseworthy. Blacks, if mentioned at all, were given in the character of childlike, rather amusing, diversions from the commonplace.

Social position did play a significant part in determining whether your wedding or demise was mentioned in the press. Men who were prominent in the professions or public life were nearly always mentioned, while veterans (especially officers) of military service usually caught the journalist's eye. As the nineteenth century progressed, tradesmen began to be included in the coverage. This 'democratization' of reporting worked its way down the ladder by the end of the century.

50

Of course unusual or gruesome deaths, and strange marriage alliances were too interesting for the newspaper people to pass over in silence. This has the effect on modern readers of suggesting a very high proportion of violent deaths and odd matrimonial alliances. Yet one cannot deny that the habit of catering to human interest did result in the recording of many hundreds of events that might otherwise have gone unrecorded.

What will you find in an old obituary or marriage notice? You will not generally find the wealth of genealogical detail that most current newspapers offer their readers, but there will often be mention of place of birth or country of origin, occupation, age, parentage of girls who were married. Depending on the individual circumstances, you may find much more, or a very brief notice — e.g., "Died, Thursday last, Mr. John Robertson, in his 65th year." Sometimes the newspaper refers to a man as an esquire. Modern misuse allows any man to have 'Esq.' written after his name, but an editor of 150 years ago had to be more circumspect. The use of 'Esq.' can be taken as evidence that the man so designated was entitled to the honour in virtue of being a barrister, a graduate of a university, the holder of certain public office, or the kinsman of a titled family.

When the **Acadian Recorder** of 5 March 1814 advised the public that Catherine, wife of Dr. Armstrong, 7th. (Royal) Fusiliers, and only child of Rufus G. Taylor, Esq., of Halifax, had died 27 November 1813 at Mount Mellick, Queens County, Ireland, it was not being anything more than factual in calling Taylor an esquire. He was a man whose social importance justified the useage.

A few newspapers have finding aids to them, and a recent publication is an actual collection of vital statistic entries. Miss Relief Williams, some years ago, prepared notes upon various subjects from eighteenth-century Halifax newspapers. Among the classes of items which she culled were the deaths and marriages and notices of settlement of estates. This last is at least an indication of the death of the person being probated. You can consult Miss Williams' scribblers full of newspaper items at the Public Archives of Nova Scotia.

The Genealogical Association of Nova Scotia has published a series of compilations of information in early newspapers. The series is called **Nova Scotia Vital Statistics from Newspapers.** Books may be ordered from Publications, Box 895, Armdale, N.S. B3L 4K5. The years covered and the prices are as follows:

1769-1812	$13.00	1813-1822	$14.00
1823-1828	$14.00	1829-1834	$14.00

Work on this series is continuing with the object of carrying it down to the mid-century.

For most newspapers, however, the researcher is on his/her own. A short list of good papers for vital statistics before 1860 is given below. Copies of most of these issues can be found in the P.A.N.S. Newspaper Room, and on microfilm in some other provincial libraries. Since marriage records improve greatly in the 1860's with the advent of sustained public registration, and since births do not get reported very generally in newspapers until the twentieth century, this list is directed mainly to material prior to Confederation.

Halifax papers predominate, which is not to say that the information in them is confined to Halifax. Most newspapers relied upon a provincial circulation and carried items from all over the province of Nova Scotia. The oldest newspaper is **The Gazette,** which appeared in 1752, and has the distinction of being Canada's oldest newspaper. This weekly changed its name in 1765 to **The Gazette or Weekly Advertiser.** Then in 1766 it became **The Nova Scotia Gazette.** In 1770 this title had the words **'and Weekly Chronicle'** tacked on. From 1789 to 1800 it was known as **The Royal Gazette and Nova Scotia Advertiser,** and then turned into **The Nova Scotia Royal Gazette.** Through all its name changes, it has continued to publish for over two hundred years, but its coverage of deaths and marriages has long been a thing of the past. Today it contains legal notices, but precious little by the way of vital statistics.

Some other Halifax newspapers with their dates are:

> **The Acadian and General Advertiser,** 1827-1834.
> **The British Colonist,** 1848-1874.
> **The (Halifax) Journal,** 1781-1799, 1810-1854.
> **Morning News,** 1842-1846.
> **The Pearl,** 1837-1840.
> **The Weekly Chronicle,** 1786-1826.
> **The Acadian Recorder,** 1813-1930.
> **The Free Press,** 1816-1834 (as **The Times** to 1848).
> **The Morning Chronicle,** 1844-1949.
> **The Novascotian,** 1824-1926.
> **The Sun,** 1845-1867.

Other Halifax papers had a religious affiliation, and their coverage was usually better for their particular co-religionists than for the public at large, though they generally printed events for all denominations. The Anglicans had **The Colonial Churchman** out of Lunenburg, 1835-1841, and later, 1848-1858, the **Church Times** at Halifax. The Baptists had the **Christian Messenger,** 1837-1884, which gave excellent coverage.

For Methodists there was **The Wesleyan,** 1838-1840; 1849-1925, while the Presbyterians had first **The Guardian,** 1838-1851, and then the **Presbyterian Witness and Evangelical Advocate,** 1848-1920. The Roman Catholics of Halifax had **The Register,** 1841-1845, then **The Cross,** 1843-1859. The only continuous Catholic paper after mid-century was begun at Antigonish in 1852; **The Casket** still exists, and a card index to obituaries is being microfilmed for the years 1852-1952. This will be available at P.A.N.S.

The main newspaper towns outside of Halifax before 1850 were Pictou and Yarmouth. Pictou had five papers before 1850. These were **The Bee,** 1835-1838; **Mechanic and Farmer,** 1838-1843; and the **Eastern Chronicle,** 1843-1953. The oldest paper was the **Colonial Patriot,** 1827-1834, founded by Jotham Blanchard, the Reformer. The more conservative could read the **Pictou Observer and Eastern Advertiser,** 1831-1835; 1838-1843. Yarmouth had one newspaper to endure from this period, namely **The Yarmouth Herald and Western Advertiser,** beginning in 1833. The **Spirit of the Times & Cape Breton Free Press** (later the **Times and Cape Breton Spectator**) ran in Sydney from 1841-1850. The **Cape Breton News** followed down to the 1870's.

This concludes what has been very much a chapter of lists. You will have enjoyed the privilege of skipping over pages of listings, and found that it was quick work to skim this chapter. It is hoped that some of you will have seen a familiar name or two among the listings, and have now an urgent desire to consult what may be a good lead. Others will find this a convenient reference for future work on their genealogy.

The chances are that whatever region or family you are working on, you will see something of use among the multitude of secondary sources that have been discussed or described for you. There is an excellent possibility that you will eventually come to the stage of working back and forth between primary and secondary sources. A place or a name which means nothing to you now may acquire great significance should you learn that an ancestor of that surname or a forebear in that place belongs to you. If you read this chapter when you knew only four or five of your ancestral family names, you may note quite a difference when you look back six months to a year from now when you will know twelve or sixteen of your ancestral names. In the course of researching the chapter, for example, I found that Crowell's coverage of the name Hovey was important to me because of new facts I had learned since last I had used Crowell's Scrapbook. A year ago, the name Hovey was just another name to me. Today, it is an ancestral lineage back to the time of James I. That is the joy and the frustration of doing your own genealogical work: you constantly make progress, and just as frequently find yourself going back to a source with which you thought you were finished. This is only one of the many ways in which genealogy is an unending search, an exciting quest, and a lot of old-fashioned hard work and thinking. To those who want all the answers, genealogy offers the challenge of trying to get them (you don't). To those who don't want all of the answers, genealogy offers the satisfaction of giving you some information. Either way, you cannot lose!

III — GETTING SOMEWHERE — THE P.A.N.S.

Secondary sources such as we have been discussing can help you to go quite far into learning about your ancestors, and in understanding the community in which the past members of your family lived. Most of the secondary source material which has been produced about Nova Scotia in the last forty years or so has benefitted from the use of primary reference materials found among the holdings of the Public Archives of Nova Scotia. These archives, hereafter referred to simply as P.A.N.S., are without a doubt the best and most comprehensive collection of Nova Scotian historical evidence to be found anywhere. Although Nova Scotia has had provision for an Archives from as far back as 1857, a proper building to house the collections dates from less than fifty years ago.

The Public Archives of Nova Scotia were housed from 1930 to 1979 in the Chase Building on the campus of Dalhousie University. In 1979 the Archives were moved to a specially designed building at the southwest corner of University Avenue and Robie Street. The building features the use of solar energy in heating and lighting, as well as climate control for storage of perishable materials.

Daytime parking in the area is restricted to two hours, and competition is tough during the university year, except on weekends. There is a small parking lot to the rear of the building which may be used in the evening. Should you prefer to write to the Archives, the postal address is **6016 University Avenue, Halifax, N.S. B3H 1W4.**

The P.A.N.S. is open every day of the year except public holidays (New Year, Good Friday, Easter Monday, Victoria Day, Canada Day, Labour Day, Remembrance Day, Christmas, Boxing Day). When these fall near weekends the Archives may be closed for several days. The customary hours of opening are:

> Sunday 1 pm - 10 pm   Saturday 9 am — 6 pm
> Monday through Friday 8:30 am — 10 pm

Xeroxing or photocopying of material can only be done by Archives' staff, and must be done between 8:30 am and 5 pm Monday through Friday.

At other times your order may be left and the copies either picked up or sent to you by mail. Delays for xerox copies are minimal, but copies from microfilm may take some time, depending upon the business of that department.

The P.A.N.S. has published an inventory of its holdings a few years ago. The **Inventory of Manuscripts** is sold out, but copies may be consulted at the Archives and in many regional libraries. The Inventory is divided into two basic groups, the RGs (Record Groups) and the MGs (Manuscript Groups). The former are the public records of Nova Scotia throughout its history, and include departmental, legal and administrative documents. The latter are papers not classified as records of the department, and include personal and church records. The Inventory tells you considerable information about each of the group of documents, although some of the MGs were too extensive to permit the complete listing of contents, and a researcher must use the more detailed finding aids which are available in the P.A.N.S. reading rooms. Even a 703 page book can contain only so much information! If you are at all able, you should carefully plan your research visits in advance. Although the Inventory is not available, this chapter will compensate for that, as will Julie Morris's short guide, **Tracing Your Ancestors in Nova Scotia,** available from P.A.N.S. for $2.95 postpaid.

The present chapter will not attempt to reprint the Inventory, but it will take the groupings from it that are of particular genealogical importance and discuss each in various amounts of detail, as required in the several cases. In general, the RGs and MGs take the material chronologically, alphabetically, or topically, so that you will usually find that there is some rhyme and reason to what at first may seem to be a daunting mass of primary material. There is a qualified research assistant on duty at the Archives in the evenings and on weekends, and several such people will be found in the building during weekdays, so that you can obtain ready assistance if you require it.

You will do much better as a user of the Archives if you will prepare yourself for your first visit by organizing your findings from family sources and the reading of secondary material. That will allow you to go to the Archives with a clear notion of what you know and what you are trying to find out. You will save yourself the loss of much time if you thrash about in disorganized confusion **after** getting to the P.A.N.S. You will spare their busy staff the trouble of trying to help someone who doesn't know what he or she wants. You cannot imagine how many people enter places such as archives and libraries and ask, even demand, to see "The Family History of the X Family," and become indignant upon learning there is nothing of that description. Then again there are the people who cannot pinpoint their ancestral home within the province because they have not really tried to do so. Make certain that you are not the one or the other; be prepared, either to ask intelligent questions or to answer them. The staff appreciates helpful researchers, understands that beginners have problems, and will make an

55

effort to assist you if you show you have done your homework and are a reasonable person.

Manuscript Groups (MGs)

The first genealogically useful section is M.G.1., **Papers of Families and Individuals**. This is very heterogeneous group of documents and information. The group divides into two parts; one for papers of individuals, the other for family papers. Below are listed all the surnames in the 1976 Inventory which have "Genealogy" marked beside them. The researcher should understand that the quantity and quality of the material is far from uniform for each. In some cases the material consists only of a page of notes or a few Bible entries, while in other cases there is almost finished product ready for publication, a major genealogical manuscript, in fact. Some listings will turn out to be the miscellaneous papers of a genealogist or boxes of notes about various families. The following individuals have "Genealogy" marked against their names:

Adams	Blair	Coates	Douglas	Giffin	Hood
Aitchison	Blakeney	Cochran	Doyle	Gillmore	Horne
Akins	Blanchard	Coffin	Drysdale	Gilpin	Horton
Allen	Blenkhorn	Cogswell	Duffus	Gladwin	Howe
Almon	Blinn	Cole	Eaton	Glassey	Hoyt
Ambrosé-Barss	Bliss	Collins	Edwards	Gordon	Hudson
Anderson	Boehner	Cossitt	Ehler	Gore	Hughes
Archibald	Boss	Cottnam	Elder	Gorham	Hunter
Aylward	Bourke	Crane	Elliott	Goudge	Huntley
Bacon	Boutilier	Crawley	Ellis	Gould	Ibbitson
Bagnell	Brehm	Creighton	Ells	Gow	Irving
Baird	Brown	Crosskill	Enslow	Grant	James
Barclay	Bulmer	Croucher	Esson	Green	Johnstone
Barnes	Burgess	Cumminger	Etter	Grono	Kaye
Barrett	Burnham	Cunningham	Evans	Handley	Keddy
Bayer	Byers	Curry	Fairbanks	Hardy	Kent
Beamish	Byles	Davidson	Farnsworth	Harrington	Killam
Bearisto	Caldwell	Dawson	Ferguson	Harris	King
Bearse	Campbell	DeLancey	Fergusson	Harrison	Kline
Beebe	Canning	Delap	Fillis	Hartshorne	Knowles
Beiswanger	Carey	Delegal	Fiske	Hatfield	Langille
Bell	Carney	Demone	Folmer	Hatt	Lawrence
Belliveau	Carty	Dewis	Foote	Hayman	Lawson
Benson	Chamberlain	DeWolf	Fox	Hebb	LeBlanc
Best	Chambers	Dick	Fraser	Hechler	Letson
Bingay	Chandler	Dickson	Frieze	Hilchie	Little
Binney	Chipman	Dill	Frizzel	Hill	Locke
Bishop	Christie	Dillon	Froose	Hilton	Lockhart
Blades	Churchill	Dimock	Fullerton	Hiltz	Lodge
Blaikie	Clephane	Doane	Gautro	Holland	Logan

Loveless	McMillan	Murdoch	Porter	Sinclair	Verge
Lovett	McNab	Murrant	Potter	Smiley	Vieth
Lusby	McNeil	Neiforth	Prat	Smith	Walker
Lyon	McNutt	Nesbitt	Publicover	Spencer	Wallace
Lyons	McPherson	Newcomb	Purdy	Spicer	Wallis
MacAulay	Mabey	Nicholson	Putnam	Spike	Ward
McCombie	Mann	O'Brien	Raine	Stairs	Waterbury
McCurdy	Manning	O'Bryan	Rand	Starr	Watts
MacDonald	Marsters	Ogilvie	Ratchford	Stevens	Waugh
MacDougall	Martell	Olding	Reid	Story	Webster
McEwan	Martin	Olmstead	Rettie	Stromberg	Weldon
MacFarlane	Mason	Page	Ritchie-	Stuart	Wells
MacGillivry	Matheson	Palmeter	Robertson	Sutherland	Wentzell
McGray	Maxwell	Parker	Robson	Tays	Wesley
MacInnes	Melanson	Parks	Ross	Theal	Whitman
MacIntosh	Miller	Pattillo	Roup	Tobin	Wickwire
MacIvor	Millett	Payzant	Rudolf	Townend	Wilkins
McKay	Montgomery	Peak	Ruhland	Trefry	Winniett
MacKenzie	Moore	Pears	Rutherford	Trost	Withrow
McKevers	Morash	Peitzsch	Rutledge	Tulloch	Wood
McKim	Morgan	Peppard	Salter	Tupper	Woodman
MacKinnon	Morris	Perkins	Sanford	Turple	Woodworth
MacLean	Morrow	Pernette	Scott	Tuttle	Wooton
McLean	Morse	Pettis	Scranton	Uniacke	Worden
MacLeod	Morton	Piers	Shaffelburg	Van Blarcom	Wrayton
McLeod	Munroe	Pineo	Sibley	Van Buskirk	Wyman
				Vaughan	Zinck

A second part of M.G.1 is that entitled "Family Papers." It is well worthwhile for you to got through the catalogue to these. Apart from the overt genealogical items, there are the materials for the construction or framework of many a family tree. In M.G.1, Box 182, for example, is a series of early assessment rolls for Horton in the 1770's. The papers of several people contain valuable collections of genealogical notes, most notably these (all in M.G.1):

Boxes 94-105 (Canon Harris) — Lunenburg Families (use with considerable care).
Boxes 109-111 (Winthrop Bell) — Lunenburg County Origins (very valuable item).
Boxes 132-133 (Bishop) — 15 books of notes on families from Kentville, Kings Co.
Boxes 367-368 (R.V. Harris) — Annapolis Families.
Boxes 817-863 (T.B. Smith) — Queens County Families.
Boxes 1008-1027 (Ells) — Eastern Shore Families (clippings, notes, letters, etc.).
Boxes 1173-1177 (Edwards) — genealogical notes for various areas of Nova Scotia.

Box 1191D (Morse) — miscellaneous genealogical notes.
Box 1469A (C.A. Johnson) — miscellaneous genealogical notes.

Certain family papers in M.G.1 have those families worked out in some detail:

Alloway (Box 1198)
Bezanson (Box 139C)
Brown of Falmouth (Box 160A)
Byles (Box 163)
Crockett (Box 996A)
Croil (Box 1162)
Croucher, St. Margaret's Bay (Box 1059A)
Curren (Box 543B)
Fraser of Middle River (Box 1210)
Fraser of New Glasgow (Box 1210B)
Fuller (Box 1250)
Gilpin (Box 329)
Hallamore (Box 333A)
Harris (Box 357, 363-365)
Hoyt (Box 483B)
Olmstead (Box 1070A)
Piers (Box 753)
Rudolf (Box 797A)
Smith, Hants Co. (Box 808C)
Strum (Box 908)
Walker (Box 1134)

Sometimes other families are traced in the papers of a listed family name in the catalogue. Here are families with genealogies filed under other family surnames:
Baker (Blauveldt Papers 1327), Bass (Lane 535), Brown (R.V. Harris 359), Bullerwell (Blaudvedt 1327), Calkin (Alloway 1198), Dennison (Chipman 181), Ditmars (R.V. Harris 357), Dore (Lane 539), Ellis (Blauveldt 1327), Fritz (R.V. Harris 357), Godfrey (Minns 574B), Harding & Hurlburt (Blaudvedt 1327), Jacques (Lane 535), Lawson (Best 128), LeBlanc (Liddell 534B), Langille & Lent (Blauveldt 1327), Lothrop (Croil 1162), MacKean (Ada MacDonald 563), Miller (Gilpin 329), Perry (Blauveldt 1327), Rae (Ada MacDonald 563), Richardson (Alloway 1198; Croil 1162), Robbins (Blauveldt 1326), Smiley (Smethurst 808B), Smith (R.V. Harris 367), Sutherland (Anslow 87), Troop (R.V. Harris 368), Wesier (Lane 539), Whitmore (Blauveldt 1327), Wile (Hoyt 483B), and Young (Blauveldt 1327; Piers 753).

The next two manuscript groups need not detain us, as they will have use only to a few genealogists, who are working on prominent individuals. M.G.2 is the papers of Political Figures, while M.G.3 is comprised of business papers. M.G.4, however, is one of the genealogical gold mines of the P.A.N.S., and bears the title: **Churches and Communities.** The two great genealogical tools among this mass of material are the church registers and the township books.

Church Records

The bulk of the church registers held in originals or on microfilm are those of various Protestant congregations between 1780 and 1914, with only a few for the time before 1780. Catholic records are even less numerous at the Archives, but many of these are the oldest, dating from the period 1679 to 1758. These are Acadian and Louisbourg records. The list of parish records which follows takes the province, county by county, then lists community church records alphabetically. The years of the registers held at the P.A.N.S. are shown, and the denomination indicated by one of the following abbreviations:

A = Anglican (closed to use, unless you have **written** permission of rector).
A* = Anglican (open to use because of age, or because rector has opened them).
B = Baptist (mostly held at Acadia University, Wolfville. See Chapter IV).
C = Catholic (mostly held by chanceries and parishes. See Chapter IV).
Cong. = Congregationalist (became part of the United Church of Canada in 1925).
L= Lutheran (in one case, A/L because the "Old Dutch Church" was Anglican & Lutheran).
M = Methodist (became part of the United Church of Canada in 1925).
P = Presbyterians (most became part of the United Church of Canada in 1925).
U = United Church of Canada (from 1925; designated as "U" when a congregation formerly Congregationalist, Methodist or Presbyterian continued from an earlier to a later date through the period of church union). Occasional notes on the registers have been provided.

ANTIGONISH COUNTY

Antigonish	A	1829-1976
	U	1854-1962
Arisaig	C	1845-1921
Dorchester	P	1821-1853
Lochaber	P	1811-1944

ANNAPOLIS COUNTY

Annapolis Royal	A	1782-1950 (typescript 1782-1888 in M,G.4, No. 4)*
	C	1702-1755 (1702-1721 published as Vol. 3, *Acadian Church Records,* ed. Milton & Norma Rieder)
Bridgetown	A	1830-1969
	M	1793-1969 (the circuit covered a wide area in early years)
Clementsport:		
St. Clement	A	1841-1973
St. Edward	A*	1841-1911 (M.G.4, No. 14)
Granville	A	1790-1801; 1814-1918
	M	1824-1831; 1920-1921
Melvern Square	B	1870s-1890s
Middleton	U	1858-1958
Rosette	A	1891-1956
Wilmot	A	1789-1909

CAPE BRETON COUNTY

Dominion	A	1906-1973
Donkin	P	1906-1908
Gabarus	M	1867-1908
Glace Bay	U	1903-1963
Ile Royale	C	1715-1721; 1726-1749; 1753-1757 (La Baleine, Lorembec, Havre St. Espirit)
Louisbourg	C	1722-1745; 1749-1758
New Waterford	A	1911-1973
North Sydney	P	1942-1967
Port Morien	A	1865-1971
	P	1900-1903; 1910-1970
Sydney	A	1785-1981
Bethel	P	1925-1974
St. Andrew	P	1815-1981
Sydney Mines	A	1816; 1848-1970

COLCHESTER COUNTY

Earltown	P	1782-1966
Economy	U	1871-1964
Glenholme	U	1892-1956
Great Village	P	1852-1872 (typescript M.G.4, No. 35)
Harmony	P	1887-1953 (listed as Valley: Harmony Church)
Londonderry	A	1865-1964
	C	1878-1909
	P	1795-1835
Lower Stewiacke	A	1850-1963
Old Barns	U	1908-1979
Stewiacke	U	1893-1956
Tatamagouche	M	1855-1956
	P	1852-1931
Truro	A	1824-1967
	B	1929-1980
	C	1873-1891; 1894-1909
	P	1834-1854
Brunswick	U	1918-1976
First	U	1873-1979

Upper Londonderry	U	1859-1965
Upper Stewiacke	P	1872-1969
Valley: Coldstream	P	1872-1972

CUMBERLAND COUNTY

Amherst	A	1822-1965
	C	1888-1909
	P	1840-1970
Beaubassin	C	1679-1686; 1712-1748 (1679-1686 published as Vol. I, *Acadian Church Records,* ed. Winston de Ville; 1712-1748 published as Vol. II, ed. Milton & Norma Rieder.)
Joggins	A	1898-1976
	C	1849-1909
Oxford	M	1883-1903
Parrsborough	A	1787-1972
	C	1853-1909
	M	1853-1972
	P	1858-1972
Port Greville	A	1897-1969
	M	1899-1972
Pugwash	A	1849-1980
	M	1875-1958
	P	1857-1895; 1906-1941
Remsheg/Wallace	A	1832-1926
	M	1831-1927
Southampton	M	1883-1968
Springhill	A	1881-1962
	C	1897-1909
Westmorland, N.B.	A*	1790-1917 (St. Mark's Church covered some of the N.S. side of the provincial boundary, e.g., Fort Lawrence and Tidnish.)

DIGBY COUNTY

Clements	A	1841-1973
Digby	A	1786-1950
Salmon River	C	1849-1907 (published)
Weymouth	A	1823-1948

GUYSBOROUGH COUNTY

Canso	A	1886-1970
Country Harbour	A	1851-1949
Guysborough	A	1786-1880
	M	1825-1907
	U	1874-1966
Halfway Cove	A	1880-1905
Liscomb: St. Luke	A	1852-1958
St. Mary	A	1852-1920 (has gaps)
Manchester	A	1847-1904
Melford/Mulgrave	A	1854-1924
New Harbour	U	1854-1955
Queensport	A	1905-1942

HALIFAX CITY

All Saints	A	1910-1974 (succeeded St. Luke's & St. Stephen's)
Brunswick Street	M	1784-1979
City Mission	M	1855-1868
Coloured People	C	1827-1835
Chalmers	P	1893-1916
Coburg Road	M	1885-1924
Dutch Church	A/L*	1783-1806 (denominational affiliation disputed)
Emmanuel	A	1893-1979 (Spryfield area)
Fort Massey	P	1875-1927
Grafton Street	M	1856-1925 (became St. David's Presbyterian)
Holy Cross Cemetery	C	1843-1944
Mount Olivet Cem.	C	1896-1944
Park Street	P	1891-1918 (succeeded Poplar Grove)
Poplar Grove	P	1843-1891 (moved to Park Street)
Resurrection	L	1914-1977
Rockingham	U	1933-1939
St. Agnes	C	1892-1919
St. Andrew's	P	1818-1979
St. David's	P	1925-1964 (building has been Grafton St. Methodist)
St. George's	A*	1813-1954 (succeeded Dutch Church)
St. John's	P	1843-1972
St. Joseph's	C	1869-1909
St. Luke's	A	1858-1910 (burned down; replaced by All Saints)
St. Mark's	A	1861-1965
St. Mary's	C	1800-1909 (originally called St. Peter's)
St. Matthew's	P	1769-1936 (indexed typescript available)
St. Matthias	A	1888-1973
St. Patrick's	C	1848-1854; 1879-1909
St. Paul's	A*	1749-1954 (Genealogical Association publishing years 1749-1768)
St. Stephen's	A	1876-1910 (succeeded by All Saints)
Salem	Cong	1868-1876
Tabernacle	B	1890-1899
Universalist	Univ	1852-1903 (gaps)

HALIFAX COUNTY

Bedford	A	1912-1969
Dartmouth:		
Christ Church	A	1793-1966
Emmanuel	A	1914-1979
St. Peter's	C	1830-1909
	M	1864-1977
	P	1833-1850
East Chezzetcook	C	1868-1909 (very scattered)
Eastern Passage	A	1867-1981
Falkland	A	1877-1977 (area generally known as Herring Cove)
French Village	A	1834-1963
Herring Cove	C	1837-1852; 1856-1909
Hubbards	A	1858-1967
Jeddore	A	1860-1953
Mid. Musquodoboit	M	1860-1943 (gaps)
	P	1848-1943

62

Musquodoboit Hbr.	A	1894-1980
North Beaverbank	P	1886-1964
Port Dufferin	A	1847-1961
Prospect	C	1823-1909 (typescript of 1823-1835 available)
Sackville	A	1813-1918 (gaps)
St. Margaret's Bay		
& Sambro	M	1820-1829; 1873-1965 (covers a very wide area)
Seaforth	A	1865-1945
Sheet Harbour	C	1857-1909
	U	1870-1979
Ship Harbour	A	1841-1982
Upper Musquodoboit	U	1882-1968
West Chezzetcook	C	1785-1890 (little pre-1815)
Woodside	A	1921-1968

HANTS COUNTY

Centre Rawdon	A	1793-1952
Elmsdale & Nine		
Mile River	P	1879-1959
Enfield	C	1857-1909
Falmouth	A	1793-1934
Hantsport	A	1892-1967
Kennetcook	P	1876-1893
Lakelands	A*	1858-1959
McPhee Corner	A	1860-1892
Maitland	A	1856-1971
Milford/Gays River	U	1870-1978
Newport & Walton	A	1793-1955
	M/P	1824-1844; 1859-1876; 1893-1926
Rawdon	A	1793-1955
	U	1926-1974
Shubenacadie	M	1870-1912
	P	1817-1840
Windsor	A	1811-1948
	C	1834-1840; 1845-1909
Fort Edward	A*	1775-1795
	M	1898-1940
	P	1873-1963

INVERNESS COUNTY

Malagawatch	P	1882-1923
Margaree	U	1823-1959
Port Hastings	U	1852-1939 (gaps)
Port Hawkesbury	U	1829-1978
Whycocomagh	P	1927-1974
Stewart Church	P	1868-1978

KINGS COUNTY

Aylesford	A	1789-1950
Berwick	A	1900-1930
	M	1864-1976
Canning	M	1856-1962

63

Cornwallis	A	1775-1969
	B	1804-1822; 1855-1875
	M	1815-1905
Grand Pré	C	1707-1748 (published in Vol. I of *Diocese of Baton Rouge Catholic Church Records.*)
	U	1819-1905
Horton/Wolfville	A*	1823-1968 (open; M.G.4, No. 18)
Kentville	A	1893-1968
Kings County	M	1819-1905 (Methodist circuit covering large area)
Kingsport	Cong	1863-1948
Upper Canard	P	1893-1962
Waterville	U	1922-1960

LUNENBURG COUNTY

Baker's Settlement	L	1899-1945
Blandford	A	1859-1929
Blue Rocks	A	1914-1964
Branch Lahave	L	1926-1963
Bridgewater	A	1854-1937
	C	1851-1909
	L	1854-1942
	U	1884-1943
Camperdown	L	1889-1946
Chester	A*	1762-1801; 1812-1859 (typescript)
	Cong.	1762-1785
Conquerall Bank/Mills	L	1889-1946
Feltzen South	L	1887-1947
Hemford	L	1888-1958
Lapland	L	1904-1946
Lunenburg	A*	1752-1942
	B	1795-1858
	L	1772-1915 (early part is in German)
	M	1815-1837
	P	1770-1969 (early part is in German)
Mahone Bay	A*	1845-1972 (1845-1870 is open)
Middlewood	L	1909-1945
Middle Lahave/Rose Bay	L	1887-1944
Midville Branch	L	1889-1970
Newburn	L	1888-1952
Newcombville	L	1906-1969
New Dublin	A*	1830-1850
	A	1867-1970
New Germany	A	1888-1973
	B	1864-1880 (see Barss Corners under Baptist Records)
	L	1900-1952
New Ross	A	1822-1943
North River	L	1899-1953
Petite Riviere	U	1847-1959
Upper Lahave	A	1884-1964
Upper Northfield	L	1901-1952

Waterloo	L	1889-1945
West Northfield	L	1889-1953

PICTOU COUNTY

Barney's River	P	1812-1883
Belfast, P.E.I.	P	1823-1849 (covers Merigomish & West River)
Blue Mountain	P	1844-1975
Caribou River	U	1888-1950
Gairloch	P	1833-1977
Greenhill	P	1864-1886
McLellan's Mountain	P	1838-1907
New Glasgow	A	1888-1969
	B	1874-1960
First	P	1908-1972
St. James	P	1786-1815; 1832-1908
Pictou	M	1872-1980
First	P	1918-1950 (succeeded Knox)
Knox	P	1850-1918 (became First Church)
Prince Street	P	1824-1908
St. Andrew's	P	1851-1980
Pictou County	P	1817-1865 (marriages only)
River John	M	1855-1956
Rogers Hill	P	1855-1907
Salt Springs	U	1941-1980
Scotsburn	P	1866-1980
Stellarton	A	1851-1975 (formerly Albion Mines)
	U	1860-1972
West Branch, East River: Hopewell	P	1827-1980
Westville	A	1897-1958

QUEENS COUNTY

Caledonia	A*	1856-1962
	C	1840-1909 (West Caledonia)
Liverpool	A	1819-1924
	B	1821-1870 (See Milton under Baptist records)
	C	1832-1892
	Cong	1792-1830; 1849-1851; 1874-1926
	M	1795-1968 (gaps)
Milton	Cong	1854-1924
Port Mouton	U	1849-1961

RICHMOND COUNTY

Arichat	A	1828-1957
Forchu	C	1741-1749
Framboise	P	1888-1905
Grand River	P	1908-1917; 1926-1980
Loch Lomond	P	1888-1972
St. Peter's	U	1924-1981
West Bay	P	1834-1975 (covers an extremely vast area)

SHELBURNE COUNTY

Barrington	A	1861-1867; 1911-1973
	B	1851-1866
	M	1790-1971
Birchtown	A	1949-1974
Churchover	A	1911-1974
Lockeport	A	1883-1974
Northeast Harbour	U	1878-1965
Roseway	A	1885-1922
Sable River	B	1841-1966
Shelburne	A	1783-1971
	M	1856-1926
	P	1828-1954
Shelburne County	M	1790-1821 (typescript available, M.G.4, No. 143)
	all	1865-1872; 1884-1919

VICTORIA COUNTY

Baddeck	A	1877-1927
	P	1914-1982
Boularderie	P	1906-1966
Cape North	U	1886-1973
Ingonish	M	1874-1965
Neil's Harbour	A	1876-1973

YARMOUTH COUNTY

Chebogue	Cong	1769-1785
Eel Brook/Tusket	C	1799-1841 (published)
Yarmouth	A	1898-1973
	P	1849-1889

In the foregoing church records, no attempt has been made here to indicate whether the records are of baptism, marriage, burial, confirmation, or acceptance. Although the churches have been listed under their several communities, the user should realize that these records, especially for the earlier periods, will have entries pertaining to people living several miles away from the particular place. Most early clergymen made circuits or parochial rounds and took weddings and baptisms wherever these services were required. Until 1832, only Anglican ministers could marry without calling of banns. Marriage licences were addressed to Anglican clergy, some of whom did pass them along to their Dissenting bretheren, but by law only Anglican clergy could dispense with banns. Many early marriages were performed by justices of the peace, but few records of such weddings have survived.

M.G.4 offers the genealogist another treasure trove besides church records. This is the series of records known as **Township Books.** The unit of local government known as a township has meant different things in various times and places. In Nova Scotia, a township was supposedly an area of 100,000 acres, or about twelve miles square, containing habitable lands. When there were fifty qualified voters, such a district could have representation in the House of Assembly. The settlers of Nova Scotia who had a background in New England of sturdy local self-government found that in practice townships in Nova Scotia were more by way of being geographical expressions than they were of local units of government.

The townships were not only a political disappointment but tended to grow up in configurations that defied the plans of government. The **Acadian Recorder** of 16 September 1854 described the situation:

> The town which was originally intended to spring up in the centre of these townships has, in many instances, not yet "begun to be;" in other cases, the only thing in the vicinity approaching to the nature of a town has persisted in growing up somewhere beyond the limits of the township. In no one instance, except perhaps that of the one containing . . . (Halifax) do these townships embody any interests, not contained in as great a degree, by the surrounding portions of the country.

One of the few things the townships did do, however, was one thing to gladden the heart of the genealogist. They attempted to keep vital records of the settling families. This was as much in the nature of keeping track of the heirs of shareholders in the township as it was anything. Rarely were these births, marriages and deaths recorded in a special volume devoted exclusively to that purpose. Most often these occurences are interspersed among other records of town accounts, cattle marks, land records, longhand copies of the grant of township, etc. The important thing is that vital records were recorded, albeit in a casual way. Sometimes the records are not as accurate as one could wish.

Sometimes the birth of a child or the marriage of a couple did not get written down in the township book. Sometimes the records seem not to have been kept for years on end. Undoubtedly, some records have been lost in whole or in part. Yet, as a source of information for the genealogist, township books are invaluable. In Nova Scotia some township books were kept for a district that had not been formally constituted a township. Some of the books record only the families that mattered in terms of proprietorship of the shares in the township. If you bear these things in mind when searching through an old book or a reel of microfilm, you will hope for the best, but not expect the answer to everything.

For a good discussion of townships and local government in Nova Scotia, try to read D.C. Harvey, "The Struggle for the New England Form of Township Government in Nova Scotia," in the **Report of the Canadian Historical Association,** 1933, pp. 15-22. Murray Beck's book, **The Government of Nova Scotia,** looks at this issue in the more general context of the development of governmental institutions in Nova Scotia over two centuries.

The following is a listing of those records of which the P.A.N.S. holds copies, and which it designates as township books. You should observe that many township books contain records for periods of time long before the settlement of the place. This is accounted for by the practice of recording the records of the settling families back to the date of the birth or marriage of the settler prior to coming to Nova Scotia. This can be very helpful in tracing the family beyond Nova Scotia back into New England, if that is where they came from. This alphabetical list is arranged to show the name of the township, the years of the vital records there, and the P.A.N.S. call number. On the next page is a map to show the location of the several townships.

RECORDS OF TOWNSHIPS

Annapolis Township	1783-1856 M.G.4, Vol. 5.
Argyle Township	1702-1913 M.G.4, micro.
Aylesford Township	1792-1855 M.G.4, micro.
Barrington Township	1764-1920 M.G.4, micro.
Chester Township	1762-1824 M.G.4, Vol. 13.
Cornwallis Township	1720-1874 M.G.4, Vol. 18,19.
Douglas Township	1784-1873 M.G.4, Vol. 25,25a.
Falmouth Township	1747-1825 M.G.4, Vol. 31,31A,31B.
Fort Lawrence Township	1766-1891 M.G.4, micro.
Granville Township	1720-1881 M.G.4, micro.
Guysborough	1782-1869 M.G.4, Vol. 109
Horton Township	1751-1889 M.G.4, Vol. 74.
Liverpool Township	1761-1870 M.G.4, Vol. 180.
Londonderry Township	1820-1840 M.G.4, micro.
Manchester Township	1782-1869 M.G.4, Vol. 109.
Newport Township	1752-1858 M.G.4, micro.
Onslow Township	1761-1841 M.G.4, Vol. 22.
Parrsboro Township	1760-1882 M.G.4, micro.
Rawdon Township	1810-1897 M.G.4, Vol. 134.
River Philip Township	1793-1860 M.G.4, Vol. 137.
St. Mary's River Twp.	1807-1856 M.G.4, Vol. 138.
Truro Township	1770-1853 M.G.4, Vol. 150, 150A.
Westchester Township	1782-1900 M.G.4, micro.
Wilmot Township	1749-1894 M.G.4, Vol. 7.
Windsor Township	1761-1819 M.G.4, micro.
Yarmouth Township	1762-1811 M.G.4, Vol. 167. (published by the Yarmouth County Historical Society, Box 39, Yarmouth, N.S., B5A 4B1, for $12.50.)

RECORDS OF DISTRICTS

Hants Co. V.Rs.	1804-1913 M.G.4, micro.
Franklyn Manor, Maccan	1755-1837 M.G.4, micro.
Windsor V.Rs.	1738-1818 M.G.1, Vol. 731A, item 87.
	1873-1890 M.G.100 — Hants County.

Although the approximate boundaries of most townships and districts have been shown here, it would be inadvisable to regard these bounds as hard and fast. These districts and townships were not generally settled from end to end, although in a good number of cases lots were laid out for settlers across the townships. Twenty-one townships elected members to the Legislature before 1859, when township seats were abolished, although four township divisions were retained in name until 1867.

I — TOWNSHIPS AND DISTRICTS IN COLONIAL NOVA SCOTIA, ca. 1825

1-Annapolis
2-Argyle
3-Aylesford
4-Barrington
5-Chester
6-Clare
7-Clements
8-Cornwallis
9-Dartmouth
10-Digby
11-Douglas
12-Economy
13-Falmouth

14-Fort Lawrence
15-Granville
16-Guysborough
17-Halifax
18-Horton
19-Kempt
20-Lawrencetown
21-Liverpool
22-Londonderry
23-Lunenburg
24-Manchester
25-New Dublin

26-Newport
27-Onslow
28-Parrsboro
29-Pictou
30-Preston
31-Rawdon
32-River Philip
33-St. Mary's River
34-Shelburne
35-Truro
36-Westchester
37-Wilmot

38-Windsor
39-Yarmouth
40-Amherst

M.G.4 is, as you can see, a genealogical collection of considerable importance, perhaps one of the two or three most significant in the P.A.N.S. Apart from church records and the township books, there are many things to delight the researcher into the several communities of Nova Scotia. You can learn much in a general way about the province's settlements by examining a copy of the P.A.N.S. publication, **Place-Names and Places of Nova Scotia.** Unfortunately, if you want your own copy, it is out of print in the original edition. However, there is a facsimile edition available for $35.00. That is a big investment in a book, unless you plan to use it frequently. The book itself is a very valuable addition to anyone's shelf of Nova Scotia.

To show what sort of miscellaneous material M.G.4 can turn up for you, there is the file on Shelburne which contains Marjorie Bruce's compilation of 496 charts showing the genealogy of twenty-nine county families. In case you should be interested, here are the names of those families:

Acker	Firth	Irwin	Nickerson
Bower	Goulden	Jones	Perry
Bruce	Hamilton	McAlpine	Ryer
Cox	Harris	McGill	Smith
Crowell	Hewitt	McKay	Snow
Davis	Hogg	MacKenzie	Swansburg
Dexter	Holden	Muir	Thorburn
Doane			

The next category of Archives records, M.G.5, is entitled **Cemeteries.** The amount of material collected for each county's burying places is a reflection of the unevenness of genealogical research and work in this province. Some fortunate counties — e.g., Colchester and Pictou — have had much work done, while others have apparently been neglected to a pathetic degree — e.g., Antigonish and Richmond. A few counties have been virtually completed and the results put on file in the P.A.N.S. Some areas have yet to attract attention or interest. Many cemeteries may have been copied and the results kept by an individual or a local group. The following list by county explains the situation as far as holdings in the P.A.N.S. are concerned:

Annapolis — almost 100% done by Dr. Marble in the 1970's; microfilm copy in P.A.N.S. Antigonish — not much done. Cape Breton — a few by Mrs. Ruth Lewis and a few for the Beaton Institute. Colchester — almost 100%; microfilm copy in P.A.N.S. Cumberland — partially in North Cumberland Historical Society publication #3. Digby & Guysborough — not much done. Halifax — almost 100% done by T. Punch in the 1970's; typescripts in P.A.N.S. Hants — J.V. Duncanson and others have done a part of the county. Inverness — scattering by Mabou Historic and Gaelic Society. Kings — being done; Douglas Eagles published those of Horton Township.

Lunenburg, Queens & Shelburne — two volumes published by South Shore Genealogical Society. Pictou — nearly 100% done by the Ritchies; some published. Richmond — Ross MacKay & Mrs. R. Lewis have deposited some records in P.A.N.S. Victoria — E. Leighton & Mrs. Lewis have put some copies in P.A.N.S. Yarmouth — Microfilm of C. Doane's work on ca. 30 cemeteries is in P.A.N.S.

Except for Colchester and Pictou counties, this copying work has been the result of a labour of love carried out without grants and without help by about eight or ten individuals. The Colchester and Pictou county work was done by equally dedicated folks, but fortunately there was enough local organization to support the work, at least in the latter stages. I think Mrs. Ruth Lewis of Halifax deserves acclaim for making a start on Cape Breton Island cemeteries. Her work is all that we have so far. The work of the Ritchies on Pictou, and Professor A.E. Marble's work in south Colchester and most of Annapolis County merits equal recognition. Anyone who has copied a burying ground really should deposit a copy of their notes in the P.A.N.S. so that others can share in a piece of our preserved and communal heritage.

The remainder of the M.G.s. really need not detain us. The genealogically valuable portion is contained in those M.G.s. we have already discussed. If someone you are interested in was involved with the Shubenacadie Canal, M.G. 24 may need your attention; society membership is covered in parts of M.G. 20. The older records of the Charitable Irish Society of Halifax (founded 1786), for instance, are very useful both in finding who was here and when, and also in some periods (e.g., 1830's) these provide a record of a man's departure from Halifax together with a notation of whither he had gone. However, the balance of M.G.s is only of use to those who need specialized information. If you have Indian, Acadian or African forebears, M.G.15 (**Ethnic Collections**) requires your study. Indians are covered from 1780 to 1867, blacks from 1798 to 1829. The growing need for genealogical material on such minorities has not been reflected by substantial recent acquisitions at P.A.N.S.

Recently the P.A.N.S. has begun to place material formerly classed as being in vertical files in a new M.G. series 100. The finding aids for this miscellaneous series afforded many sources of interesting information. One example will show what may be found. M.G.100, Vol. 102, item 31, is a series of genealogies of Hampton, Annapolis County, made ca.1972 by Mrs. J.N. Dexter. The 27 families are Allen, Anderson, Anthony, Beardsley, Corbett, Cropley, Easson, Farnsworth, Fash, Foster, Gaskill, Grant, Graves, Hall, Healy, Hill, Mitchell, Neaves, O'Neal, Poole, Roach, Risteen, Rumsey, Slocomb, Snow, Titus and Young.

Record Groups (RGs)

The other, more official, half of the P.A.N.S. holdings is the Record Groups (R.G.s). There are nearly fifty of these, but we shall examine the fourteen which I consider to be the most beneficial to the genealogical researcher.

R.G.5 is made up of the "Records of the Legislative Assembly of Nova Scotia." One part of this group is Series "E," which contains some polling lists and poll books. More interesting are the records contained in R.G.5, Series "P," the **petitions** received by the Legislature between 1816 and 1926. Earlier petitions for the period 1802-1815, are catalogued in the P.A.N.S. publication, **A Calendar of Official Correspondence and Legislative Papers Nova Scotia, 1802-1815.** Some classes of petition are temperance (from ca. 1850), agriculture, grants of money, communications, education, poor relief, shipping, roads and bridges, trade and commerce.

Our ancestors did not hesitate to draw up a document in which "We, your humble petitioners" proceeded to ask for whatever at the moment "We" felt needed to be done, and invariably they would "humbly sheweth" their reasons. There are two genealogical sources in the petitions submitted to the Nova Scotia Assembly. There are the valuable lists that can be compiled by a study of signatures on a petition. You can find out who was living where and when. Sometimes you may have an ancestor who was living in 1819 and whom you know was dead by 1838. That would entail a massive newspaper search without the guarantee that he ever had an obituary in the first place. But if you can find the man's signature on a petition dated 1831, you have cut down your odds appreciably. Secondarily, or even primarily, some petitions happen to contain considerable information about the suppliant if he is asking as an individual for something from the government.

Here are some examples and appetizers drawn from R.G.5, Series "P." Among the Agriculture items in Volume 52 is a petition of 1833 from Miles McDaniel of Margaree, Cape Breton. He describes his career in the Island from 1807 when he emigrated thither from Ireland. Twenty-one of his neighbours signed in support of his plea.

Communications petitions include windfalls such as those of Volume 57: a petition of 1820 signed by thirty-six residents of Porter's Lake, asking aid to open the lower end of the lake to the sea, the passage having been silted up. Again, from 1825, twenty-eight residents along the Roseway River in Shelburne asked government assistance. Examples abound, and I would venture to say that all parts of Nova Scotia, if not every community in it, are to be found somewhere among these petitions.

Poor relief petitions in Volume 80 supply such gems as one of 1817 from Kings County, which is marvellously well written and contains masses of names of residents. General petitions included in Volume 3 include one from 1827, signed by the freeholders of Shelburne. The scroll (for such it amounts to) is very lengthy, and must represent a substantial part of the freeholders.

Roads and bridges are the greatest source of names, since they got signed by virtually everyone in the district, since roads were desired by Tory and Reformer alike, and almost everyone got into the act of asking. Some petitions are almost like directories in that they were taken or sent down the road. The resulting order of signatures is not an unreliable guide of who lived next to whom. Volume 93 contains an item that caught my eye. It was the petition of my ancestor, John Rafter of Sherbrooke Settlement, in Lunenburg County (this was on the Annapolis Road in one of the military settlements erected after the Napoleonic Wars). It seems that the bridge over a neighbourhood river had been washed away by ice in January 1829. On 12 February, Rafter, supported by two road overseers who vouch for him, offers to build a new bridge in a better place, to be 100 feet long and 15 feet wide, supported by three piers of wood. He will build for £40., and warrant his work for seven years. It concludes with a lovely firm signature. When I could read, in the man's own handwriting, his sensible plan for a new bridge and his logical explanation of the reasons why the former one had been swept away, it made that man seem real to me for the first time. How otherwise would I have gained such an insight into what sort of person he had been?

The petitions repay the time it takes to search them with diligence and patience. Perhaps the best way to attack such a mountain of paper is the casual approach. Regard them as so much interesting reading material, and chip away gradually at the pile. If you are in a hurry, it is easy to keep a watching brief for placenames, so that you can put the document aside if it is not for the right area, and go on to the next one. I suspect, though, that he who takes the time to glean will harvest more than he who rushes headlong through the collection. Each of us knows the time we wish or may put at the disposal of ancestor seeking. But for goodness' sake, do sample at least one or two petitions just to get the flavour and the feel of the times. You can't regret it!

The next category, R.G.7, is made up of volumes 217-221, and is called the **Provincial Secretary's Papers.** These have possible value in that they allow you to see if your ancestor was a holder of one or more of forty-six different offices under the government. These county officials were very important in the lives of their neighbours and you might get some insight into the status of a forebear by looking at these lists of road overseers, fence viewers, and constables. From these and other sources, the P.A.N.S. is now compiling alphabetical files of commissions, and you would be well advised to ask to have these indexes checked for any surname in which you are interested.

Census — Poll Taxes

The first census taking in Nova Scotia was carried out by French officials in the later seventeenth century. After the founding of Halifax in 1749, the British also became interested in keeping a count of the population of Nova Scotia. A very valuable tally of population was taken in the province on the eve of the American Revolution, with one or two districts being taken later. Then, efforts at census taking ceased until after the Napoleonic Wars had ended. Censuses were taken about once a decade from 1817 until Confederation. Since the unification of Canada in 1867, a census has been taken at least decennially, the series beginning in 1871. At the present time, the 1871 and 1881 census records are open to public scrutiny and historical research. Census records from 1891 onwards are not available at present. All census records at P.A.N.S. are listed under R.G.12, although some of the individual returns fall in other record classifications.

French censuses include those of 1671 (6 pp., Acadia); 1678; 1686 (28 pp., Acadia); R.G.1, Vol. 2, doc. 28, 1693 (28 pp., Acadia); 1695; 1698; 1699-1700; 1701; 1703; 1707; 1708. In 1714, just after mainland Nova Scotia became officially British, another tally was made for Port Royal and Minas (8 pp., R.G.1, Vol. 3, doc. 55). French censuses for Ile Royal date from 1715; 1716; 1717; ca. 1720; 1724; 1726; 1728; 1734 (of the heads-of-family type). A census by LaRoque (1752) amounts to 172 pages, and covers both Cape Breton and P.E.I. It was published in the **Report of the Canadian Archives,** Vol. II, 1905.

Let us examine the census records between 1752 and 1871 in greater detail. In 1752, a population return was made for Halifax and vicinity. The area covered was basically the town of Halifax and its immediate environs, with one or two islands reported outside of those in Halifax Harbour. The information is arranged in six columns, as follows: 1. Heads of families; 2. Males above 16; 3. Females above 16; 4. Males under 16; Females under 16; 6. Total. This return forms an appendix to T.B. Akins' "History of Halifax City," **Collections of the N.S.H.S.,** VIII. Taken in conjunction with the 1749 passenger lists of Cornwallis' expedition, and with the 1750 victualling list for Halifax (appendix B to the **Report** of the P.A.N.S. for 1941), this source can provide a very fair idea of who were among the earliest English-speaking settlers of Nova Scotia. Anyone comparing the three lists will be struck by the high rate of turnover, as very many of their initial party of settlers died off or moved away quickly.

The next attempt to count the population was made in 1770, and provides us with quite a good nominal roll of pre-Revolutionary Nova Scotians outside of Halifax town. A few townships were counted at later dates, but 1770 forms the bulk of the results. These returns are arranged in columns headed: 1. Names of the Master or Mistress of the Family; 2. Numbers in each family (men, boys, women, girls); 3. Total Persons; 4. Religion (Protestants, Roman Catholics); 5. Country of Origin (English, Scots, Irish, Americans, German and other foreigners, Acadians). Americans meant people born in North America outside Nova Scotia, while Acadians in one case — Annapolis — is used to mean anyone born in Nova Scotia. The returns were made by township, for the following places:

1770 — Amherst, Annapolis, Barrington, Cumberland, Falmouth, Granville, Hillsborough, Horton, Londonderry, New Dublin, Onslow, Pictou or Donegall, Sackville, and Truro.

1773 — Yarmouth.

1775 — Conway.

1787 — Queens County (gives number of men, women, children, totals only).

This group of returns has been published twice, the first time being as appendix B to the **Report** of the P.A.N.S. for 1934. This was indexed in issue seven of the **Genealogical Newsletter** of the N.S.H.S. Then, in 1972, the Chicago Genealogical Society, brought these two together under one cover, **Nova Scotia 1770 Census.** Interestingly enough, R.G.1, Vol. 443. the source of these returns, contains another township return that has not been published, perhaps because a fragment was missing, and perhaps because there was not absolute certainty of its location. I have studied that document and compared the names in it with church, land and probate records, and have not the slightest doubt that it represents about 98% of the return for Lunenburg Township. Another good source for early Lunenburg names is the 1757 victualling list, published as an appendix to the **Report** of the P.A.N.S. for 1935.

Father François Lejamtel took nominal censuses of his territory in 1793 (lost) and in 1809. The latter, covering Chéticamp and Margaree can be found on pp. 291-5 of Anseleme Chaisson's **Chéticamp: Histoire et Traditions Acadiennes.**

Two census returns from Cape Breton between 1811 and 1818 are the first for the Island under British rule. That of 1811 is incomplete, but it does cover parts of all four modern counties. The headings in the return include: 1. Head of Family; 2. Occupation; 3. Age and sex breakdowns; 4. Cattle, sheep, horses, vessels; 5. Stations (i.e., where settled). Rather more of the 1818 census survives. Its information is of considerable value. Headings include: 1. Heads of Family; 2. Age; 3. Time on the Island; 4. Country; 5. Country of Parents; 6. Situation (i.e., where settled); 7. Trade; 8. Married or Single; 9. No. of Children. In one part of the 1818 return the researcher will see under "Country" the words N. Britain or North Britain. This refers to Scotland, and occasions no difficulty here. However, you will sometimes find a headstone or newspaper obituary in which a person is referred to as a native of such-a-place, N.B. The name of the community will generally be

75

the clue, but there will be times when you will have to investigate whether the man came from St. Andrews, New Brunswick, or St. Andrews, North Britain.

CENSUS RECORDS, 1752-1787

1752 - Halifax, Ile Royale
1770 - Amherst, Annapolis, Barrington, Cumberland, Falmouth, Granville, Horton, Londonderry, Lunenburg,
New Dublin, Onslow, Pictou, and Truro.
1773 - Yarmouth.
1787 - Queens Co.

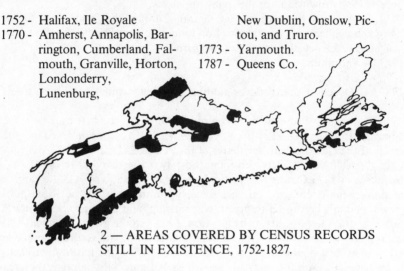

2 — AREAS COVERED BY CENSUS RECORDS STILL IN EXISTENCE, 1752-1827.

CENSUS RECORDS, 1809-1827

1809 - Cheticamp & Margaree.
1811 - Cape Breton Island.
1818 - Cape Breton Island.
1817 - Antigonish, Guysborough, Hants, and Pictou.
1827 - Cumberland & Halifax Co.; Townships of Annapolis,
Antigonish, Argyle, Barrington, Clare, Clements, Liverpool, Shelburne, Wilmot, and Yarmouth; Districts of Bras d'Or & Louisbourg.

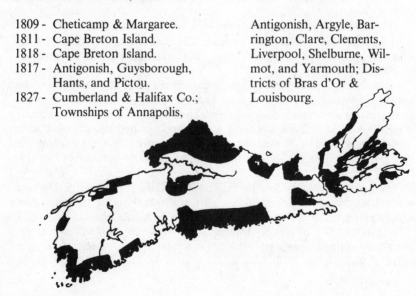

The eleven pages of the 1811 return and the twenty-two of 1818 together form Appendix A to **Holland's Description of Cape Breton Island,** published as its second publication by P.A.N.S. in 1935. It is out of print, but many Nova Scotian libraries have a copy.

Meanwhile, in 1817, a census had been taken in mainland Nova Scotia, but little of it has survived. R.G.1, Vol. 445, documents 6 to 8, supplies the returns for Hants, Pictou, and Sydney (Antigonish and Guysborough) counties. Hants and Pictou returns show heads of household, rough age-sex breakdowns, and total. Sydney County tells rather more: 1. Head of Household; 2. Number in Family; 3. Country of Origin (English, Scots, Irish, American, German and others, and Acadians (i.e., born in Nova Scotia). A list of the inhabitants of St. Margaret's Bay, Halifax and Lunenburg counties dated 27 June 1817 is in R.G.20, Series "C", Vol. 88, item) 174. I believe this may be a draft document of a census tally. It tells head of family, numbers of men, women and youths above 12, children, servants.

Around this period, the outstanding emigré priest, Abbé Jean-Mande Sigogne, had charge of the Acadian mission at St. Mary's Bay. At least twice, 1818-1829 and 1840-1844, Sigogne compiled a listing of his parishioners. This is a very valuable source for the district of Clare. Equally valuable is Sigogne's return of 1816-1819 for his parish of St. Anne and St. Pierre, Argyle. The P.A.N.S. has this on microfilm.

In 1827, the first census was taken of all of Nova Scotia. It gives: 1. Head of household; 2. Total in family; 3. Number by sex; 4. Occupation; 5. Religion; 6. Births, marriages and deaths in the year previous to the census. Halifax County (but not the town), Cumberland County, Louisbourg & Bras d'Or districts survive, as well as the townships of Annapolis, Argyle, Barrington, Clare, Clements, Liverpool, Shelburne, Wilmot and Yarmouth. The 1827 census, plus that of 1818 for Pictou was published by P.A.N.S. (Allan Dunlop). A fragment of Halifax Town, found by the author, appears in the **Genealogical Newsletter,** No. 36, pp. 80-82. Antigonish County returns were going moldy, so they were very carefully transcribed and the original disposed of. The copy has been published as an appendix to the 1938 **Report** of the **P.A.N.S.**

The 1838 census of Nova Scotia is the first nearly complete survival from among early population counts. Only Cumberland County is missing. Fortunately, that county survived from the 1827 census. This census is available on microfilm, and will give the following information: 1. Head of Family; 2. Occupation; 3. Age-sex breakdown; 4. Totals. The totals tend to be confusing since sometimes the head of the family is included in the total but is not entered in a column as an adult over 14, so that the tally seems inaccurate. If the total is one less than the numbers severally for the family, the usual explanation is that the head of the family is omitted from the numerical breakdown. Check the arithmetic of a few other families on the

77

same return, and if the "one extra" phenomenon is uniformly found, you can safely assume that the one missing from the detailed age-sex figures is the head of the family.

The 1851 census (R.G.1, Vols. 451, 452) survives for three counties — Halifax, Kings, Pictou. It gives head of family and an age-sex tabulation. Occupations and religion are reported, but a user must read very carefully to match these to names. You must use this census on microfilm.

The 1861 census was the last provincial return before Confederation. This is the first to survive for the entire province. It gives the head of the family, an age-sex breakdown in some detail, occupation and religion, with various returns relating to manufactures and livestock. Religion is often calculated by district rather than by household, so the use of that part of the return is diminished.

Finally, there is the 1871 census, the first federal one. It gives the name, sex, age, birthplace, religion, ethnic origin, occupation, marital status, and certain other information about every individual person in the province. The P.A.N.S. has microfilmed copies of the entire Nova Scotia portions of this census. The 1881 census may also be consulted and offers the same details.

Poll Taxes

A poll tax or, as it was sometimes called, a capitation tax, was a small levy raised by charging a sum of money from each adult male (i.e., men above the age of 21 years) in a district. Theoretically, then, a poll tax should provide a comprehensive directory of all such persons within a district. In practice, people were inevitably missed because they lived in remote areas, were inadvertently bypassed, or lived in areas of disputed jurisdiction. It would be reasonable to assume that in rural areas where ready cash was scarce and even one shilling was a large sum, some younger men pretended to be 20 or 19 to avoid being listed and having to pay the tax. These are useful records, indeed, for the genealogist, especially do they gain in value when you consider that between 1770 and 1827 or even 1838 no other list of similar completeness exists. The P.A.N.S. hold a good series from 1790-1796, though 1791-1795 are the dates of all but two poll taxes now preserved. These are the districts (with years for which poll taxes are extant, sometimes with a year or two missing from the series) that are available:

Amherst 1791-1795 (Cumberland Co.)
Annapolis 1792 (Annapolis Co.)
Argyle 1791-1795 (Yarmouth Co.)
Aylesford 1791 (Kings Co.)
Chester 1791-1795 (Lunenburg Co.)
Clements 1791 (Annapolis Co.)
Cornwallis 1791-1795 (Kings Co.)

Digby 1795 (Digby Co.)
Douglas 1791 (Hants Co.)
Economy 1793-1795 (Colchester Co.)
Falmouth 1791-1795 (Hants Co.)
Fort Lawrence 1792-1794 (Cumberland Co.)
Halifax 1791-1793 (Halifax Co.)
Horton 1791 (Kings Co.)

Liverpool 1792-1794 (Queens Co.)	Truro 1791-1795 (Colchester Co.)
Londonderry 1791-1795 (Colchester Co.)	Wilmot 1791-1794 (Annapolis Co.)
Lunenburg 1793-1795 (Lunenburg Co.)	Windsor 1791-1795 (Hants Co.)
Maccan and Nappan 1791-1794	Yarmouth 1793 (Yarmouth Co.)
(Cumberland Co.)	Musquodoboit 1791-1793 (Halifax Co.)
River Hebert 1791-1794 (Cumberland Co.)	New Dublin 1791-1795 (Lunenburg Co.)
River Philip 1791-1795 (Cumberland Co.)	Newport 1791-1795 (Hants Co.)
Shelburne 1791-1794 (Shelburne Co.)	Onslow 1791-1795 (Colchester Co.)
Shubenacadie 1795 (Colchester & Hants Co.)	Queens 1791-1795 (Queens Co.)
Stewiacke 1795-1796 (Colchester Co.)	Rawdon 1791-1795 (Hants Co.)
Tatamagouche 1794-1795 (Colchester Co.)	Remsheg (Wallace) 1790-1795

Other nominal returns include Country Harbour, Guysborough, Canso, Manchester, Tracadie, Pomquet, Pictou, Antigonish, Merigomish, Havre Bouche, Crow Harbour, and Gulf Shore.

Neither lists nor related documents seem to be about for Barrington, Clare, Dartmouth, Granville, Kempt, Parrsboro, Preston or Cape Breton. Of course, as Cape Breton was not then part of Nova Scotia, this is not surprising, though what has happened in the other cases is a seeming loss of the entire record.

The map on the next page shows the geographical pattern of the surviving lists.

R.G.13 contains the records of **Customs Dept.** These are not of great genealogical value, but may prove of secondary importance, as they may help in determining what ships from whence arrived within a certain period of years. Port records are held from the early nineteenth century for Halifax, Pictou, and Wallace. Passenger lists do not occur here, but in R.G.18, while citizenship records come under R.G.49.

Education is the title of R.G.14, along with **Schools.** School papers for the nineteenth century are arranged in order of county, so that you must know the county in which the community was located before you can use these records. Many of the school records of the 1820's to 1840's give the names and approximate ages of the pupils, together with their father's or guardian's name, and thus they assume great genealogical value and significance. However, do regard ages shown for children as very approximate; in my experience, some runs of records will allow a spread of as much as four years in the date of a child's birth — e.g., William X is given as age 6 in 1829 returns, and as age 12 in 1833, and age 15 in 1834. That particular boy was baptized in July 1822, age 3 months!

Four province-wide school censuses of the twentieth century are held at the P.A.N.S. These list all school age children in each district with birthdate and parents' names. Those for the years 1937 and 1946 are complete for the province, while those for 1958 and 1961 each lack a county, Annapolis and Colchester, respectively. These more recent records are not generally open to public use, though Archives staff will probably be willing to check them for a specific name or two.

3 — SURVIVING POLL TAX RECORDS FROM THE 1790'S.

Explanation of Numbers

1 - Amherst
2 - Annapolis
3 - Argyle
4 - Aylesford
5 - Chester
6 - Clements
7 - Cornwallis
8 - Digby
9 - Douglas
10 - Economy
11 - Falmouth
12 - Fort Lawrence
13 - Halifax
14 - Horton

15 - Liverpool
16 - Londonderry
17 - Lunenburg
18 - Maccan & Nappan
19 - Musquodoboit
20 - New Dublin
21 - Newport
22 - Onslow
23 - Queens
24 - Rawdon
25 - Remsheg (Wallace)
27 - River Philip
28 - Shelburne
29 - Shubenacadie

30 - Stewiacke
31 - Tatamagouche
32 - Truro
33 - Wilmot
34 - Windsor
35 - Yarmouth
36 - Manchester
37 - Guysborough
38 - Country Harbour
39 - Havre Bouche & Tracadie
40 - Antigonish
41 - Pictou Harbour

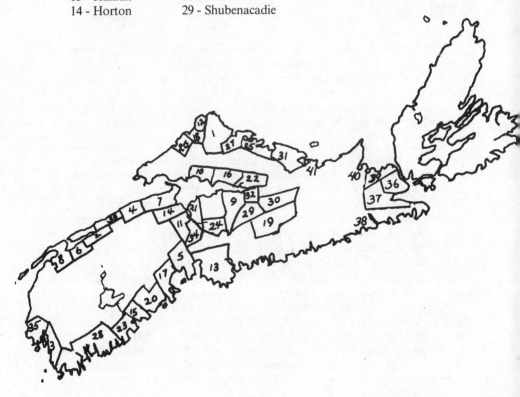

80

The next important record group for genealogy is R.G.18, which includes **Immigration.** The passenger lists are disappointingly few. If you can do so, you will find it worth studying J.S. Martell's short P.A.N.S. publication, **Immigration to and Emigration from Nova Scotia 1815-1838,** and its continuation, 1839-1851, by Mrs. R.G. Flewelling, in **Collections of the N.S.H.S.,** XXVIII. These will give you some idea of the numbers coming to Nova Scotia, and where they were coming from, and landing when they arrived here.

The surviving passenger lists come from a variety of sources, including original lists, contemporary and later copies, and secondary sources. They should not be accepted uncritically. In addition to individual passenger lists for vessels, the P.A.N.S. has ten reels of microfilmed passenger lists for vessels reaching Halifax, 1881-1900. R.G.18, Series "A", contains naturalizations and oaths of allegiance taken between 1862 and 1915. See R.G.49 also in this regard.

Chronologically arranged, here are the ships for which the P.A.N.S. has passenger lists, dating from pre-1867. The arrangement is ship's name and year of arrival here, port of embarkation and arrival, who was aboard the vessel.

Date	Name of the Vessel(s)	From Port of . . .	to Port of . . .	Who Was Aboard?
1638	Saint Jehan	La Rochelle	Port Royal	French
1749	Alexander, Baltimore Beaufort, Brotherhood, Canning, Charlton, Everley, Fair Lady, London, Merry Jacks, Roehampton, Wilmington, and Winchelsea.	London	Halifax	Cornwallis's English to found Halifax.
1750	Ann	Rotterdam	Halifax	"Foreign Protestants"
1751	Gale, Murdoch, Pearl, Speedwell	Rotterdam Rotterdam	Halifax	"Foreign Protestants"
1752	Betty, Gale, Pearl Sally Speedwell	Rotterdam	Halifax	"Foreign Protestants"
1760	Charming Molly	Boston	Annapolis Royal	New England Planters
1773	Hector	Greenock	Pictou	Scots
1774	Albion	Hull	Fort Cumberland	Yorkshiremen
	Two Friends	Hull	Halifax	Yorkshiremen
1775	Durham	Newcastle	Halifax	Yorkshiremen
	Jenny	Hull	Nova Scotia	Yorkshiremen
1783	Union	Huntington Bay	Nova Scotia	Loyalists
1784	Argo	East Florida	Guysborough	Loyalists
1801	Dove, Sarah	Port Williams	Pictou	Scots
1808	Clarendon	Oban	P.E.I.	Scots
1815	Prince William	Sutherlandshire	Pictou	Scots
1818	Two Brothers	Wales	Shelburne	Welsh
1828	St. Lawrence	Newcastle	Port Hawkesbury	English

Date	Name of the Vessel(s)	From Port of . . .	to Port of . . .	Who Was Aboard?
1841	Lady Gray	Cromarty	Pictou	Scots
1843	Catherine	Tobermory	Canso Gut	Scots
1848	Ellen	Loch Laxford	Pictou	Scots
	Hope, London, Lulan	Glasgow	Pictou	Scots
1862	Alma, British Queen,	Liverpool	Halifax	English
	Frank Flint, Morning Star,			
	T. and J., Thomas			
1864	Europa	London	Halifax	English and Irish
	Kedar	Liverpool	Halifax	English and Irish
	Euroclydon, Indian Queen	...	Halifax	English and Irish

The P.A.N.S. has also some lists of Scots arriving in 1802, 1815-1816. I can add eight more lists or parts of lists to the foregoing, from material found in the Archives or acquired by them when these lists were drawn to their attention:

1760	Lydia	Newport, RI	Falmouth	New England Planters
	Sally	Newport, RI	Falmouth	New England Planters
1767	Betsy	Philadelphia	Pictou	Philadelphia Settlers
1775	Providence	Newcastle	Halifax	Yorkshiremen
	Squirrel	Poole	Halifax	English
1799	Polly	Belfast	Halifax	Ulstermen
1803	Commerce	Greenock	Pictou	Scots
1839	Aide-de-Camp	Ireland	Halifax	Irish (partial list)

All published passenger lists may be located through Filby & Meyer, **Passenger and Immigration Lists Bibliography, 1538-1900.** The first three volumes of immigrant names have been purchased by Genealogical Association of Nova Scotia and placed in P.A.N.S. for consultation.

The usefulness of newpapers to researchers is well illustrated in this last case. **The Novascotian,** 27 June 1839, p. 306, carried the card of thanks on behalf of the passengers on the "Aide-de-Camp" to Capt. John Innis. John Baird and Joseph Hamilton, cabin passengers, signed, as did James Barris, Michael Cam, Robert and Thomas Carbery, Michael and Richard McLaughlin, and John McFarlane on behalf of the steerage passengers. A like notice appeared in **The Novascotian,** 5 June 1843, thanking Capt. Samuel Edwards of the brig "Eagle." Careful reading of the newspapers of the period will probably unearth other partial passenger lists, to be gleaned from the signatories of the notices in the newspaper.

R.G.20 is the collection of papers to do with Lands and Forests. The "A" section is entitled **Land Grants and Petitions,** and is extremely important as a genealogical tool. The P.A.N.S. has a large alphabetical file of draft land grants and petitions from the settlers asking for land. These have been indexed on cards and cross-referred by Archives staff to provide a convenient aid for researchers. There are two chronological parts, 1775-1799, and 1800 onwards. Many petitions recite information about the petitioner, his family, his country of origin, date of coming to Nova Scotia, indicate previous military service or land grants in the province. It is commonplace to find the age of the Petitioner or the names of his children in such a record. One only wished all settlers had petitioned for land, but this of course was not the case. As a rule of thumb, note that petitioners fall into two broad categories: those who were needy, and those who felt they had some claim on the bounty of the government — e.g., Loyalists.

There are a few further details you should know about these files, and about how to follow up your findings in them. Once lands were granted and passed into private hands, the subsequent transactions connected with the land would be recorded in the files of one of the twenty-one land registries in Nova Scotia (See R.G.47, below). The Crown Lands Dept., Dept. of Lands and Forests, 3rd Floor, 1740 Granville St., Halifax, N.S. has a series of 140 maps showing the first land grants in each district, on a scale of one inch to 80 chains (which, at 66 feet to the surveyor's chain, comes out to 1" = 1 mile). So, if you can locate a grant in the files and then geographically, you can probably obtain a map to show the grant and the adjoining lands for $1.05 (tax included) from Crown Lands. The P.A.N.S. also has a microfilm index of land grants, spanning over two hundred years.

To illustrate the valuable information to be found on the index cards, here are a few examples from actual cards on file. Early settlers from Scotland appear often, as witness this case from 1815. John McKay and others, recent emigrants from Sutherlandshire, Scotland, were living at Pictou, and were so poor and needy that they were crammed three and four families to a "house." Then, to delight the genealogist, comes a choice and informative list of the petitioners: John McKay, 25 single; Alexander McKay, 27, married; Alexander McKay, 30, wife, 5 children — Rachel, 8, William, 6, James, 4, Thomas, 3, and Mary, 4 months; Donald Murray, 22, wife, children — Christiana, 4, Margaret, 2; Alexander Sutherland, 27, a soldier, and his sister; William Douglas, 30, wife, 1 child; Donald Douglas, 22, his mother, 2 girls and 2 boys; Widow McKay, 30, with four girls and a boy age 12; William Sutherland, 20; John Murray, 16, and his two sisters. There seems a good chance that these 35 people are the better part of some ship's passenger list. The petition is dated from Pictou, 10 Nov. 1815. No doubt an enthusiastic historian could discover the name of the vessel which brought these Scots to Nova Scotia.

Another group coming here after the Napoleonic War was the Irish. In 1819, Daniel Oats, who had emigrated here from Ireland three years earlier, was married to the widow of William Nash, who had eight children. By her, Oats now had a child. The petition lists the offspring: Ellen 19, John 16, Thomas 14, William 12, Eliza 10, Tobia 8, Catherine 6, and Robert Nash 4;

and Maria Oats 1. Curiosity about this one led me to another card, the petition of William Nash in 1813. He was an Irishman who had lived for 15 years in Guysborough, and had a wife and seven children. He received a grant of 500 acres on 2 July 1813. When the two cards are taken together you can see how much information has been gained without much trouble.

Yet another group of settlers at that time were the refugees from the Chesapeake Bay area, people who had left slavery under the banner of freedom to live in freedom under the banner of empire. In 1825, Clement and Charles Bennett, "Negroes," asked land on the road between Preston and Musquodoboit. They state in their petition that they had come to Nova Scotia during the late American War, i.e., during the War of 1812.

Sometimes quite a few points come from a land record. The petition of John Blades **et al.** of Cobequid Road, 1828, mentions Blades, William Whippy, and others. We find that James Johnson, 42, was an immigrant from "Fenmara" (This should read Fermanagh), Ireland, in 1819. When you consider Fermanagh's location in Ireland, you have a hint that Johnson travelled here from Londonderry on one of the two ships reported as reaching Halifax from Derry during 1819: the 'Halifax Packet' (made port, June 1819), or the brig 'Frances-Ann' (arrived July 1819). John Kerr is also mentioned as an immigrant from Ireland, but two years out. Another man is called John McKitchin, otherwise McMikel. This could be a very vital clue, if it suggests a name change is taking place.

One final instance in the petition of 1815, which gives three generations of one Acadian family. Francis Bellfountain, a native Nova Scotian, living at Chezzetcook, had a wife and five children (Charles 10, Mary 8, Margaret 6, Sally 3, Ephraim 10 months). They were living in a log house on a lot that had been granted the petitioner's father, John Bellfountain, in 1785. Francis sought to claim the 200 acres granted his father and since escheated (i.e., had reverted to the government, either for want of improvement being made, or because no legal heir had been found.)

I hope these examples will convince you that the Land Papers ought to be checked. Once you get the name and date of the petition, it is possible to request the original document for examination. Within minutes you may be holding in your hands the self-same piece of paper on which your several times greatgrandfather wrote a signature or made his "X" with awkward care. Apart from the possibility that the entire document may afford more information than does the index card, there may be a small thrill as you realize that there, in your palm, is tangible evidence of your personal heritage! Savour the moment, for such are rare enough, but remember too that everything people said in their old petitions was calculated to pry something out of the government, and people frequently exaggerated their age, claimed children who had been married and under their own roofs for years, and extenuated every circumstance to the limit. My sentiment about old petitions is gratitude to the generations of librarians and custodians who kept the papers safe from harm, theft or destruction. If a moral is to be found, it is our common duty to share in conservation and perservation of old records and new.

The "B" section of R.G.20 is the **land records of Cape Breton.** The best single source here is a large typewritten volume entitled "Calendar of Cape Breton Land Papers 1787-1848." Here, in one indexed book, are over 3300 petitions and so forth to do with land in Cape Breton. The early years are rather lean pickings, and some years in the late 1700's have no entries (1788, 1791, 1793, 1799), and the collection thins out after 1840. This source is as informative as the series "A" material. To give just one example, the 1817 petition of John Westray, age 35, tells that he was born in England, had lived twelve years in Halifax, and was now in Cape Breton with his wife, Ann, and five children — Isabella, Mary Ann, Margaret, Fletcher, and Sarah.

Only R.G.22 need detain us long from the next dozen records groups. R.G.22 is described as Militia (Nova Scotia). Among these **military records** there are various muster rolls, including for examples the following: Clare and Digby, 1814-1846; Clementsport 1860-1866; Halifax 1807, 1870; Guysborough 1860's. One volume, number 376, contains muster rolls of Loyalists (1784) and military settlers at Annapolis, Digby, Merigomish, Pictou, and Wallace. These rolls give names, classes of people, numbers in their families, where they settled, what corps they had belonged to, etc. Useful in this collection is P.A.N.S. publication number four, **Loyalists and Land Settlement in Nova Scotia.**

Moving along to R.G.32 we find ourselves once again in a collection of great interest to the genealogist. This contains **Vital Statistics** and, in particular, the marriage records of Nova Scotians. This group comprises government registration of births, deaths, and marriages/marriage intentions. Before 1849 the only records are the **Marriage Bonds.** These bonds were an indication of an intention to marry, and in all cases an attempt should be made to find some records (e.g., church register, Bible entry, newspaper announcement) to indicate that the marriage subsequently took place. Many of the bonds were returned with the date of the wedding and the minister's signature endorsed. Surviving Marriage Bonds for 1763, 1765, 1770-1780, 1782, 1784-1799, 1801-1850, 1854-1856, 1858-1864 are held by the P.A.N.S. A microfilm series has many of these bonds arranged alphabetically by groom's names. No cross reference by bride's name exists. The bonds frequently give the groom's trade or occupation, while witnesses and sureties were often relatives of the parties planning marriage.

In 1864, the Nova Scotia government made a serious attempt to register vital statistics, and for about a dozen years this effort had some success. The first year or two were a time of adjusting to the change and probably the registrations were far from complete, but for 1867-1874 the coverage was quite thorough, then tapered off until 1877 when the birth and death registration lapsed. The P.A.N.S. hold the scanty birth registration (R.G.32, Vol. 5, 87), but the main value is found in the marriage and death records. These are arranged by county and year in two series, one for deaths, one for marriages. There is a typed index to Pictou deaths 1864-1877.

A death record will often give the name and the age of the deceased person, his birthplace and residence, and sometimes his parentage. In the case of an 80-year-old dying in 1868, the record that gives the parentage and birthplace must be regarded as very significant. A marriage record will generally give the name, age and occupation of the married parties, their parentage, birthplace and residence, marital status, and the place and date of the wedding.

Recently, the P.A.N.S. received the marriage license records for the period from about 1849-1851 until 1906-1918 from the Deputy Registrar-General. These form R.G.32, Series "M." A microfilm index is nearly complete in its coverage, and researchers can use these and the finding aids, to locate the licenses they wish to see. The index shows two numbers, one before and one after the name of the married person. The one in front of the name is the reference by which the P.A.N.S. has filed the marriage documents. In some cases the small slip which contains the best information is missing from an envelope. They have probably been missing for years and there is little you can do about it except to copy the remaining information and try to get a church record or newspaper notice of the marriage and hope that these provide you with more information.

The cut-off date for each county's marriage licenses at the P.A.N.S. depends on when the old index ceased. Here is a list to show the cut-off date for each county. Anything after the year shown must be sought from the Deputy Registrar-General. The dates are:

Annapolis	1908	Guysborough	1906	Pictou	1917
Antigonish	1910	Halifax	1916	Queens	1910
Cape Breton	1912	Hants	1916	Richmond	1918
Colchester	1914	Inverness	1908	Shelburne	1908
Cumberland	1913	Kings	1909	Victoria	1918
Digby	1909	Lunenburg	1908	Yarmouth	1908

R.G.32, Series 'WB' is on microfilm and provides the information found in the provincial registers of births and deaths from 1864 to 1877. Births formed 29 old volumes and fill almost thirteen reels of film, arranged by counties. Deaths accounted for 20 of the former volumes and take up something over five reels of microfilm, again set forth by counties and years.

R.G.35 consists of **municipal records,** such as assessments, minutes of councils, polling lists, and lists of county officials. The P.A.N.S. has some, though very few, polling lists and voters' lists. Halifax County for 1914 and 1916 are held, as well as several from Hants East from the 1880's and 1890's. Stray survivals from other areas do turn up sometimes. I've noticed one from 1894 for Inverness County, another for Port Morien, Cape Breton, 1928, and a third from 1900 for North East Margaree. You can check the Inventory at the P.A.N.S. under R.G.35, Series "E" to see if any new lists have turned up. Series "A" in this group is the Halifax City and County Assessments. For the town and city, the earliest is from 1817, and many are available from then until 1841. Except for 1862, there is then a gap until 1890. The county of Halifax assessments are held from the 1830's, 1840's, and 1890's.

R.G.41 is useful in certain instances, if you are looking for gruesome details of a sudden death. This group is made up of the Coroner's Inquests and Medical Reports, and is incomplete. There are a few from as far back as the 1790's, and a scattering in the present century, but the great mass date between 1820 and 1900.

There are two very important groups of records at the P.A.N.S., which will be discussed in more detail in the next chapter. These are Registry of Deeds (R.G.47) and Court of Probate (R.G.48). The value of wills and inventories, deeds and mortgages to the genealogist is fundamental, inasmuch as these are among the documents everyone will think about when they start to research a genealogy. The indexes to deeds are quite useable, and generally there are two, paged alternately, by either the name of the Grantee (i.e., purchaser) or that of the Grantor (i.e., seller). The index to wills can be tricky, in as much as **all** estates are indexed together, and only by examining the microfilm of the appropriate county and numerical reference can you discover whether there was a will or not. Using the microfilm index to some probate court records (e.g., Halifax County) is among the most trying experiences I've had in doing Nova Scotian genealogy, since when the papers were microfilmed several years back, the photographer neglected to check that he showed the estate reference number for each file filmed. As the alphabetical arrangements were a bit bizarre, finding something in the microfilm index can be very time-consuming and frustrating, If possible, better visit the appropriate courthouse and arrange to see the file of the estate you want to examine.

The following table sets forth jointly the deeds and probate documents held at the P.A.N.S. To help further, I have added a column to show when each county was formed and, where applicable, shown the previous jurisdiction for the present county or district. Generally mainland counties were under Halifax offices until organized locally, while those on Cape Breton Island came under Sydney offices. Records after the dates shown must be sought at the several county courthouses.

WILLS AND DEEDS AT THE P.A.N.S.

County: Subdivision	*Date of Formation	Deed Dates	Will Dates	Original Estate-Papers	Previously part of the County of . . .
Annapolis	1759	1763-1910	1879-1970	1763-1900	Halifax
Antigonish	1784	1785-1907	1821-1963	1819-1900	Halifax
Cape Breton	1784	1786-1910	1802-1969	1782-1902	...
Colchester	1835	1770-1903	1770-1969	1800-1900	Halifax
Cumberland	1759		1796-1969	1764-1900	Halifax
Amherst		1764-1904			
Parrsboro		1789-1905			Kings
Digby	1837	1785-1910	1810-1970		Annapolis
Guysborough	1836				Halifax
Guysborough		1785-1910	1942-1967		
Sherbrooke		1815-1910	1855-1969		
Halifax	1749	1749-1903	1749-1968	1749-1871	...
Hants	1781	1763-1906	1761-1968		Kings
Inverness	1835	1825-1910	1831-1969	1830-1906	Cape Breton
Kings	1759	...	1783-1968		Halifax
Aylesford		1820-1843			
Cornwallis		1764-1903			
Horton		1766-1843			
Lunenburg	1759	...	1762-1967		Halifax
Chester		1879-1908			
Lunenburg		1759-1912			
Pictou	1835	1771-1905	1811-1969	1813-1901	Halifax
Queens	1762	1764-1920	1768-1970	1765-1901	Lunenburg
Richmond	1835	1821-1909	1941-1969		Cape Breton
Shelburne	1784	...	...		Queens
Barrington		1854-1913	1868-1969	1784-1900	
Shelburne		1783-1921	1785-1970	1766-1900	
Victoria	1851	1851-1911	1856-1968	1852-1901	Cape Breton
Yarmouth	1836	1766-1910	1794-1970	1794-1900	Shelburne

*The "Date of Formation" in all but two cases is that when the county was by law established. Halifax County was established in 1759, but until that time all the mainland came under the jurisdiction of Halifax. Cape Breton County dates from 1820, but the Island of Cape Breton as a separate government dated from 1784. More information about the organization of the counties of Nova Scotia may be gained from Dr. C. Bruce Fergusson's pamphlet, **The Boundaries of Nova Scotia and its Counties,** Archives bulletin number 22 (1966).

The last R.G. that requires special notice is R.G.49, **Citizenship Records.** Records of citizenship for seven communities in Nova Scotia are held in this classification. Apart from Halifax City, the six jurisdictions with the date on which each record begins, are:

Digby 1901; Kings 1916; Lunenburg 1916; Pictou 1918; Shelburne 1903; Truro 1922.

Now that we have toured the M.G.s and R.G.s of the P.A.N.S., we have still three other useful sources at that institution which remain to be examined. The first of these is the **Biography File.** This consists in a series of drawers full of index cards, alphabetically arranged, of miscellaneous information about many Nova Scotians from many sources, collected by Archives staff for sundry purposes over many years. The facts may come from a newspaper notice, an oral interview, a letter, or almost anywhere. It is a source worth your checking under any surname in which you are interested. In a row with this file is the **Community File,** where references to material about any community is readily retrievable.

A second source is the unique set of county maps drawn by Ambrose F. Church, a nineteenth-century surveyor and cartographer in Nova Scotia. **Church's maps** show almost every house within each county, with the name of the head of the household. This latter is often enough misspelled, so be prepared to find a name that looks almost like that for which you are searching. Comparison with land grants sometimes helps in identifying descendants of the original grantees, especially where land passed down in the family, but without documentation. The oldest map of a county is that for Halifax (1865), and the most recent that for Queens (1888). Others with dates are Pictou 1867, Digby and Yarmouth 1870, Hants 1871, Kings 1872, Cumberland 1873, Colchester 1874, Annapolis and Guysborough 1876, Cape Breton 1877, Antigonish 1878, Shelburne 1882, Lunenburg, Inverness, Richmond and Victoria between 1883 and 1887. C. Bruce Fergusson wrote a biographical sketch of the man, "Ambrose F. Church and his Maps," which appeared in the **Journal of Education** (June, 1970). The inset township maps were numerous on Church's maps, and Dr. Fergusson provides the full list in the article just mentioned. Taken in conjunction with early directories, these maps are very valuable genealogical aids. Copies may be ordered from The Dept. of Lands & Forests, Box 698, Halifax (B3J 2T9), or Maritime Resources Management Service, Box 310, Amherst (B4H 3Z5).

Directories and almanacs are handy references and the P.A.N.S. has a good collection. **Cunnabel's City Almanac and General Business Directory** of 1842 is the earliest source for many names of ordinary citizens of Halifax, and its exceptional appearance was probably inspired by the incorporation of Halifax as a city in 1841. Richard Nugent had a business directory in 1858-59, and Luke Hutchinson produced one for 1863. From 1869, McAlpine's directories became annual, and soon were listing the names, occupations and addresses of all employed adults in Halifax and Dartmouth.

For the province at large, Hutchinson had directories for 1864-65 and 1866-67. Lovell produced one in 1871, and McAlpine printed others for 1890-97, 1902, 1907-08, and 1914-15. McAlpine also produced a huge maritime provinces directory for 1870-71. A good run of directories can be an appreciable help to the family historian in tracking branches of the family who remained inside a known general area. That for 1890-97 gives useful clues to the parentage of like-named individuals, e.g., "Simon Landry, S's son, Seaman, Descousse."

Among the delights of browsing in an Archives as opposed to researching, there is the marvellous variety of odds and ends one comes upon by chance. Over the years each of us gets a list of such miscellaneous material. Much of the list we'll never use, but we keep the reference anyway, just in case . . . ! Here, in order of place, are thirty-three such things. You just might be interested in someone in one of the places, and this stray reference could help you, so here goes.

PLACE	TYPE OF RECORD	P.A.N.S. HOLDING
Arichat, Richmond Co.	Electoral directory 1933-34	R.G.5, Series E. Vol. 36. Nos. 7,8
Baddeck, Victoria Co.	Assessment Roll 1911	R.G.35, 323 (A.2)
Chester, Lunenburg Co.	Proprietors 1802	M.G.100, Vol. 120, No. 36
Cornwallis Twp., Kings Co.	Assessment list 1765	M.G.1, Vol 181, folder 4, item 13
Cumberland County	Graham's Parrsboro Families	Microfilm — Mrs. A.L. Graham
Digby Township	Grantees 1800	M.G.100, Vol. 135, No. 5
East River, Pictou Co.	Inhabitants 1789	M.G.100 Vol 137, No. 12
Gulf Shore, Cumberland Co.	Genealogies early families	Stack 15, Nos. 121, 181 (Gulf Shore)
Guysborough	Grantees 1784	M.G.100, Vol. 148, No. 11
Halifax City	Allotment Book 1749-86	Microfilm
Horton Twp., Kings Co.	Assessment Roll 1765	M.G.1, Vol 181, folder 4, item 11, 12.
Jeddore, Halifax Co.	Loyalist Muster Roll 1784	Microfilm
Liverpool, Queens Co.	McLeod genealogies	Microfilm
Londonderry, Colchester Co.	Genealogies 1775-1900	Microfilm
Lunenburg	Passenger lists 1750-52	M.G.4, No. 83
Minudie, Cumberland Co.	Tenants lists 1768, 1843	M.G.100 Vol. 190, No. 32
Musquodoboit Valley	Logan's notes on families	M.G.100, Vol. 194, No. 42
New Dublin, Lunenburg Co.	Wainwright's genealogies	M.G.4, No. 117
Newport, Hants Co.	Vital statistics 1860-95	M.G.100, Vol. 196, Nos. 24, 27
Nova Scotia	Elderly people 1888 (Names suggest Colchester Co.)	M.G.100, Vol. 200, No. 19
Pereau, Kings Co.	Genealogies 1890	M.G.100, Vol. 205, No. 13
Port Medway, Queens Co.	Letson's genealogical notes	M.G.4, No. 128
Preston, Halifax Co.	Blacks at Preston 1833	M.G.15, Vol. 9, No. 56
Queens Co.	Genealogical clippings	M.G.4, No. 131
Rawdon, Hants Co.	Vital statistics 1864-78, 1903	Microfilm
Sackville Twp., N.B.	Township book 1748-1871 (Some N.S. material is included)	Microfilm
Shelburne Town	Town lot holders 1784	M.G.100, Vol. 220, No. 18
Shelburne Co.	Assessments 1786-87	M.G.4, No. 140
	Muster Books of free blacks, 1784	M.G.100, Vol. 220, No. 4

Sydney River, C.B. Co.	Assessments 1850	M.G.100, Vol. 236, No. 13
Wallace Bay,	Brown, McKim, Tuttle,	Microfilm
Cumberland Co.	Wells, gen.	
Yarmouth Co.	Doane's genealogies	Microfilm
Whole Province	Card Index	Genealogy File, 12 drawers

In this chapter I have attempted to impress on the genealogist the enormous value that the Public Archives of Nova Scotia must have for anyone who is thinking of working on a family history in Nova Scotia. The sheer mass of material is quite overwhelming, but careful reading over of the chapter, together with reference to the index, should enable you to discover sources which you could investigate for further information about any family that may have lived in this province. Indeed, I am sometimes so taken with the P.A.N.S. that I have to make an effort to recall that there are other institutions in the province which have much to offer.

IV — GETTING HELP AROUND THE PROVINCE

The Public Archives of Nova Scotia is the single most important emporium of genealogical lore in the province, but it is not a monopoly. There are many valuable records held elsewhere in the province, and there are numbers of helpful societies and individuals available to help you. How well you are received will depend in part on whether you have carried out your part of things and organized your findings and checked secondary sources **before** expecting smaller local libraries and private people to help you.

The County Courthouse

The preservation of land and probate records falls within the jurisdiction of the municipalities. Both types of record provide the genealogist with considerable data. They are surprising in their variety, often supplying information that one would not expect to find there. Legal researchers and experienced genealogists may get maximum use from probate and land records, but many laymen do not.

The land registry comprehends a body of material that ranges from mortgages and deeds to leases, liens, releases of mortgage, orders of court, sheriff's deeds, and wills in which real estate is bequeathed. Technically the law requires the registration of every instrument by which ownership of realty changes hands. This can be stretched in practice to include personal documents such as deed polls, and deeds of co-partnership. Deed polls are much more common in Great Britain, but are a legal means of registering a change of name, individual or business.

Many land records include maps or plans of premises, subdivisions, or even entire districts. Some plans show several persons of the same surname on adjacent properties. If these are compared to a grant of land, it may be found that these are often co-heirs of a first grantee. Depending upon the time elapsed since the grant, it can be supposed the owners shown on a plan were related to the grantee as sons, brothers, grandsons, nephews, or whatever. In an area such as Cape Breton or Antigonish where some surnames are very common, any clue to relationship is essential to the solution of a family tree.

Information that is generally available on deeds includes the date, names, addresses, occupation and wife's name of grantor and grantee, a description of the land and the names of witnesses, actual and memorial. Genealogically speaking, land transactions have the value of mentioning relatives who formerly owned the transferred lands. Deeds sometimes quote the date and instrument (including grants) by which the grantor obtained title to the land. This frequently offers hints to the family's length of residence in the area. Sometimes deeds speak of former residents as being "now of . . . ," thus telling us where that person has gone. Likewise, addresses of present residents may add "formerly of . . . ," and thereby tell us whence they have come. Use of terms such as Mr., Esq., gent., should be noted. These were not used indiscriminately until the present century and therefore afford clues to a man's social status in his lifetime.

The naming of someone in the land records also provides the hint to check the voters' lists and assessments for the appropriate area, where such records exist. Indeed, the two sources should be checked in any case, since many land instruments — especially before 1900 — were not registered. Assessments or voters' lists may be the only means of turning up rapidly a landowner who does not, for one reason or another, appear in the index to the deed books.

It may be necessary also to search the records of more than one municipality, as the bounds of counties and townships were not always in their present location. All of mainland Nova Scotia was in Halifax registry district until 1759. Nearly two dozen districts now exist (see list in chapter 3). Margaret Burns Martin offers a list in her article, "Deeds and Documentation of Early Nova Scotian Buildings," in the Nova Scotia Museum publication **The Occasional,** III, 1 (Summer, 1975).

Deeds require a double index, one by grantor (ventor, seller, lessor), the other by grantee (buyer, leasee). Besides naming these parties to the transaction, indexes may tell the transfer number, the year of registration (and note well that this is often not the same as that of the instrument; sometimes the time lapse is forty years), book and page numbers; perhaps the location of the land; and the type of instrument. The grantor's name may be followed by a code number to indicate whether the grantor acted alone, with others, or on behalf of others. For example, one finds deeds by grantor **et ux.** (and wife), **et al.** (and others), **et vir** (and husband), in his own name as executor, trustee, attorney, or in someone's name as executor of, attorney of, or trustee of, that other person. The indexes are a valuable finding aid, but how much the searcher gains from their use depends in good measure upon his observing carefully the various points just mentioned. One must also warn researchers to look for spelling variants of any name in the index, as the index was made liberally to the spelling on the instrument, and if the document reads BRUN for BURN, the index will do the same. When a deed is made by a grantor **et al,** the latter may be a listing of the heirs of someone or other.

A last point to mention regarding deeds and land transfers is their negative value, in what they don't say. If "A" conveys lands to "B," wife of "C" for $1.00, "in consideration of the natural affection" he bears her, it is fair to assume that "A" and "B" are related, likely as father and daughter, or as brother and sister. Land records to about 1910 are held at the P.A.N.S. as well as in the several county courthouses. Those after 1900 can be found only in the courthouses, during normal business hours. There is generally a nominal fee for searchers, such as 50¢ or $1.00 for a day.

Probate registration in the Maritimes began in Halifax began in 1749. Today there are twenty probate courts in Nova Scotia, and as many more in the other Maritime provinces. It has been the exclusive concern of government from the start, which marks a significant break with British tradition. In Britain, until 1858, probate authority was vested in the ecclesiastical courts of the established Church of England.

The sort of records created by the probate of an estate depend upon whether the deceased person had made a will (was testate), or had left no testamentary writing (was intestate). Although technically a will deals with real estate, and a testament with personality (clothing, furniture, stock, money, tools of trade), I shall use the words "will" and "testament" interchangeably as is the common practice. Occasionally, for reasons that were sufficient at the time, a will was made orally by a dying person to credible witnesses. Such a will, known as a nuncupative, is today valid only in the case of men in active service. Once such a record is written down and sworn, it is treated much the same as any other will.

A will must be "proved" — i.e., one or more of the witnesses to the signing of the will demonstrate to the satisfaction of the probate court that the document presented for probate truly is the will of the deceased testator. Without the existence of a will matters are more complicated, both because the disposition of the property is subject to the rules governing descent of property, and because so much more has to be done in paperwork. The first step in an intestacy is the filing of a letter of administration (Admon. for short), usually by one of the natural heirs — the spouse, child or sibling of the deceased person. Besides wills and Admons. there is a vast range of materials that finds its way into probate files. Nova Scotia's Probate Act alone instances more than thirty set forms that could be required, with as many as a dozen of them possibly included in one probate. Of course, for the researcher each new paper is a source of potential new clues, so I suppose the proliferation of documentation is not a loss. The application for probate now must show the place and date of death. Sometimes the court appoints a guardian **ad litem,** naming therein minors who have an interest in an estate. This is helpful in cases where property is bequeathed to all the children of the deceased in equal shares, but the number and names of the offspring is not mentioned in the will or the Admon.

I will conclude these general remarks about probate by advising anyone who seeks the details of Nova Scotian inheritance law to consult the Descent of Property Act, the Wills Act, the Probate Act, and the Trustee Act. Jointly, these will answer almost any question likely to occur to the researcher seeking guidance through the confusing toils of this branch of legal knowledge. Statutes of earlier times will perhaps enlighten the student concerning the rules and regulations then in force.

Wills are, of course, the most desirable probate documents. They contain a mine of personal information about the testator and his circle, once any legal verbiage is cut through. Most wills name several members of the family, give a good idea of the testator's position in life, and accurate detail of residence and possessions, and a rough idea of date of death. Wills do not meet everyone's ideas of egalitarianism, however. While some ordinary farmers and tradesmen did make wills, most did not. Probate records reflect the fact that it was the officials, officers, merchants and gentry that made wills, partly because they were the people who owned enough property to need a will, and partly because ordinary people often arranged matters within the family without creating a written document "to make it legal." Until the 1880's, female testators were uncommon, and were almost always spinsters or widows, and rarely married women. Some of the most informative wills were those of elderly spinsters who itemized meticulously bric-a-brac for each of their grandnieces and nephews by name, often with genealogically helpful phrases such as "to my grandniece, Minnie Irving, daughter of my nephew, Hugh Murray of River St. Mary" or to "Jane, Ellen and Maud, the three daughters of my brother, Samuel Shaw, deceased."

There is much to remember when you make an abstract of a will. You want, beside the obvious finding aid of an estate number or will book and page number, these other details: full name and address of testator, his job or status, the date of signing the will and any codicils, the date of probate (this may be years after the date of the will), the names of executors and witnesses. As for the body of the will, you will need the name and stated relationship of everyone named in the will, possibly the location of property bequeathed, and anything else that attracts your attention. Bear in mind that terms of relationship may not be what, literally, they are today.

Sometimes the main beneficiary of an estate is barely mentioned in a will. The inexperienced researcher may see a will that leaves £50 to this one, and 20 acres to that one, and decide that the person named at the end got little of anything. That is an error, since more often than not the last-named was the residual legatee — the one who got everything not specifically bequeathed to someone else. An estate worth £18,000 could stand many £50 bequests before it was seriously depleted. Another case of care is with persons left a shilling or a dollar. This expression alone does not deam disinheritance; more usually it indicates that the child so mentioned has already been provided for, when married or on coming of age.

Let me conclude in the hope that these remarks will help you with wills and deeds at the county courthouse. The researcher has to keep his or her eyes open to every possible clue, and the archivist, librarian or genealogist who is consulted by the family historians is obliged to impress upon beginners that care is necessary. The family historian has many treats in store if he will persevere and be cautious. An inventory that itemizes the ancestral property piece by piece will tell you much of your ancestor's circumstances. Until about 1840, these inventories were painstakingly made — e.g., "one kettle . . . 6d.; one pair of tongs . . . 4d." You should get more than names and dates from early probate records and land records.

Church Repositories

We have seen that the Public Archives of Nova Scotia has a large collection of church registers in originals and on microfilm. The reader will have noticed, too, that Anglican and Presbyterian records formed the larger share of the P.A.N.S. holdings. **Anglican** churches in Nova Scotia are all within the Diocese of Nova Scotia, whose archives are situated at 5732 College Street, Halifax (B3N 1X3). Genealogical material is not held there, except coincidentally, but that office can help you to get the name and address of the clergyman in many congregations throughout the province.

The **Baptist** records are held by the various congregations or placed for safe-keeping in the Maritime Baptist Archives, Vaughan Library, Acadia University, Wolfville (B0P 1X0). There is a published catalogue to the Maritime Baptist Historical collection (1955), and a revised edition is planned in the next few years. The following parish registers are held at Acadia:

Advocate Harbour	1839-1890	Bridgewater	1848-1886
Antigonish	1823-1900	Canning	1882-1903
Avonport	1876-1909	Free Baptist	1850-1906
Barrington		Centreville	
Central	1859-1912	Digby Co.	1836-1862
Christian Bethel	1811-1878	Shelburne Co.	1821-1866
Providence	1907-1928	Chegoggin	1892-1905
Second Free	1878-1897	Clementsport	1825-1911
Temple	1878-1897	*Cornwallis	1778-1806
Barrington West	1848-1863	Falmouth	1843-1934
Barss Corners	1842-1913	*Florence	1906-1922

Bear Point	1866-1944	Gaspereaux	1857-1886
Berwick	1829-1858	Greenfield	1858-1949
Bridgetown	1838-1888	Guysborough	1848-1919
Halifax (First)	1835-1864	*Scotch Village	1799-1911
Hebron	1837-1915	South Ohio	1859-1928
Indian Harbour	1843-1885	South Rawdon	1823-1894
Londonderry	1903-1926	Springhill	1904-1931
Maitland & Noel	1891-1909	Summerville	1859-1903
New Tusket	1843-1885	Tusket	1911-1949
Milton, Queens Co.	1823-1913	Upper Canard	1816-1877
North Brookfield	1828-1917	Upper Stewiacke	1839-1868
Onslow	1791-1869	West Bay	1869-1890
Onslow West	1868-1881	Weymouth Bridge	1902-1903
Paradise and	1827-1949	Weymouth North	1809-1867
Clarence		Windsor	1879-1881
Port Clyde	1943-1950	Wine Harbour	1897-1907

*these three have gaps.

Acadia Library advises that the following genealogically useful items are held in their collections, apart from the Baptist church records. They have the township books for Horton and Parrsborough townships, and voters' lists and school records from Kings and Annapolis counties and Cornwallis township. There are a few Bibles which contain family records, and a number of letters, diaries and journals having some genealogical value. One has been published recently. **The Diary of Joseph Dimock** contains Baptist marriages at Chester, 1794-1845. Their archives are open Monday to Friday from 8:30 am to 5 pm, and you may do your own research there or enlist the help of their most obliging staff.

Presbyterian congregations retain their own records and have no particular central archives, so that applications must be made to the several clergymen and congregations. You can get help in locating the records by writing to the appropriate clerk or presbytery. There are three in Nova Scotia: Presbytery of Cape Breton, Box 184, Baddeck, Victoria Co., N.S. (four island counties). Presbytery of Pictou, 139 Almont St., New Glasgow, N.S. (northern and eastern mainland). Presbytery of Halifax and Lunenburg, 67 Russell St., Dartmouth, N.S. (western mainland).

The **United Church of Canada** has the Maritime Conference Archives, Pine Hill Divinity Hall, 640 Franklyn St, Halifax, N.S. (B3J 3B5). The archivist is Rev. N.A. MacLeod, and the archives are available weekday mornings, 9-12 am. Though no appointment is needed, you would be well advised to notify them you plan to come on a certain date. They have very few registers, letters, diaries and journals, but they can supply information as to the whereabouts of the registers of the United Church congregations, many of which pre-date church union in 1925.

The **Roman Catholic Church** in the province has three dioceses. The metropolitan see of Halifax governs Colchester, Cumberland, Halifax, Hants, Lunenburg and Queens counties. Yarmouth diocese contains the counties of Annapolis, Digby, Kings, Shelburne, and Yarmouth. Antigonish diocese controls Cape Breton Island and the three mainland counties of Antigonish, Gusyborough, and Pictou. Addresses of the Chancery Offices are:

Archdiocese of Halifax, Box 1527, Halifax, N.S. (B3J 2Y3).

Diocese of Antigonish, Box 1060, Antigonish, N.S. (B2G 2L7).

Diocese of Yarmouth, 43 Albert Street, Yarmouth, N.S. (B5A 3N1).

Policy varies for each diocese. Antigonish Chancery has no custody of registers, so you must approach the particular parish and seek help. The older parishes in that see are Antigonish, Arichat, Arisaig, Boisdale, Bras d'Or, Bridgeport, Broad Cove, Brook Village, Chéticamp, Christmas Is., D'Escousse, East Bay, Guysborough, Havre Boucher, Ingonish, Johnston, Judique, L'Ardoise, Main-à-Dieu, Mulgrave, North Sydney, Pictou, Pomquet, Port Felix, Saint Andrew's, St. Margaret's, Southwest Margaree, Stellarton, Sydney, Tracadie, and West Arichat. Any parish that I have approached has been helpful, so if you write the parish priest and enclose a self-addressed stamped envelope, you should have a fair chance of getting a reply. Patience is necessary, for priests tend to be quite busy men.

The Yarmouth Chancery has church registers, an old journal, cemetery inscriptions, and some secondary material. The researcher is expected to carry out his own work, and should make an appointment for a weekday between 9:30-11:30 am, or 2-4:30 pm. Older parishes in the diocese are Amirault's Hill, Annapolis Royal, Church Point, Comeau Hill, Digby, Kentville, Meteghan, Plympton, Pubnico, Quinan, Salmon River (published for 1849-1907) Ste.-Anne-de-Ruisseau, St. Bernard, Wedgeport, and Yarmouth

The Chancery Office, Archdiocese of Halifax, holds many older registers, but that office advises that its records are not available. Some records were microfilmed by the Mormons years ago, and you can write to them for help. Recently the P.A.N.S. has been allowed to microfilm the Catholic registers, and the Archdiocese agreed to allow the public to consult the microfilm held at the P.A.N.S. These registers generally end about the time that Civil Registration began in the province, so that there is generally little necessity to consult more recent church records. The Chancery has retained registers for St. Joseph's Orphanage, 1895-1954; and for St. Patrick's Home, 1885-1952.

The records for other denominations are held by the various congregations in each area. Those persons having ancestry in Nova Scotia that is Adventist, Congregationalist, Jewish, Lutheran, Quaker, Sandemanian, Universalist, and so forth, must determine the location of the church body to which their forefathers adhered, and then arrange to see any records that may exist. Most denominations have marriage records, and burial/death records are general. Baptism, or records of joining a church are also customary. Some, such as Catholics, Anglicans and Lutherans, kept good records of confirmation, while these, Presbyterians, and Methodists were inclined to keep records of communicants. Lists of pew holders can sometimes also be found to be of genealogical value as corroborating evidence for someone's date of birth or continuing to live in a certain community.

Historical Societies and Museums

There can be no substitute for detailed local knowledge, and researchers into the Nova Scotian past, genealogical and otherwise, are fortunate in there being a network of interested organizations in the province. The overall organization is known as the Federation of Nova Scotia Heritage, whose executive director and offices are situated at Suite 305, 5516 Spring Garden Road, Halifax, N.S. (B3J 1G6). The following list is a selection of the many societies and museums in Nova Scotia. These have been selected as being most likely to help those doing genealogical research. There are probably others that are as good, but I have no word from them and no contact with them, so I cannot speak of them. To facilitate reference, I have listed the groups alphabetically within seven large regions, on the principle that, failing help from one, you can try another society within the same general area.

CAPE BRETON ISLAND (Cape Breton, Inverness, Richmond, Victoria Counties):
Acadian Museum, Cooperative Artisanale de Chéticamp Ltée., Box 98, Chéticamp, N.S. (B0E 1H0).
Beaton Institute of Cape Breton Studies, College of Cape Breton, Box 5300, Sydney (B1P 6L2).
Chestico Historical Society, Box 149, Port Hood, N.S. (B0E 2W0).
Ingonish Historical Society, Box 46, Ingonish, N.S. (B0C 1K0).
Inverness Historical Society, Box 161, Inverness, N.S. (B0E 1N0).
La société historique acadienne de l'Isle Madame, Box 60, Arichat, N.S. (B0E 1A0).
Mabou Gaelic & Historical Society, Box 175, Mabou, N.S. (B0E 1X0).
Old Sydney Society, Box 912, Sydney, N.S. (B1P 6J4).

EASTERN MAINLAND (Antigonish, Guysborough, Pictou Counties):
Canso Historical Society, Box 189, Canso, N.S. (B0H 1H0) Mr. Neil MacIsaac, President).
Guysborough Historical Society, Box 140, Guysborough, N.S. (B0H 1N0).
Hector Centre Trust, Box 1210, Pictou, N.S. (B0K 1H0).

99

Pictou County Historical Society, 86 Temperance St., New Glasgow, N.S. (B2H 3A7).
Pictou Heritage Society, Box 364, Pictou, N.S. (B0K 5R4).

HALIFAX COUNTY
Chezzetcook Historical Society, Box 89, Head Chezzetcook, N.S. (Mrs. Florence Wilmshurst). (B0J 1N0).
Cole Harbour Rural Heritage Society, 1754 Cole Harbour Rd., Dartmouth, N.S. (B2W 3X7), (Mrs. Rosemary Eaton).
Dartmouth Heritage Museum, 100 Wyse Rd., Dartmouth, N.S. (B3A 1M1).
Marine Highway Historical Society, c/o Mrs. Grace Forsythe, R.R.#2, Head of Jeddore, N.S. (B0J 1P0).
Sackville Heritage Society, 73 Caudle Park Cres., Lower Sackville, N.S. (B4C 1Z5).

SOUTH SHORE (Lunenburg, Queens Counties; Shelburne Municipality):
Lunenburg County Historical Society, LaHave, Lunenburg Co., N.S. (B0R 1C0) (Mrs. James Creaser).
Lunenburg Heritage Society, Box 674, Lunenburg, N.S. (B0S 2C0).
New Ross District Museum Society, New Ross, Lunenburg Co., N.S. (B0J 2M0).
Parkdale-Maplewood Museum, Barss Corner, R.R.#1, Lunenburg Co., N.S. (B0R 1A0) (Mrs. L. Wentzel).
Queens County Historical Society, Box 1078, Liverpool, N.S. (B0T 1K0).
Shelburne Historical Society, Box 39, Shelburne, N.S. (B0T 1W0).
South Shore Genealogical Society, Box 471, Bridgewater, N.S. (B4V 2X6).

WESTERN MAINLAND (Barrington, Yarmouth and Clare):
Cape Sable Historical Society, Box 42 Crowell P.O., N.S. (B0W 1S0).
La Société Historique Acadienne de la Baie Ste-Marie, St. Anne's College Church Point, N.S. (B0W 1M0).
Weymouth Historical Society, R.R. #1, Plympton, N.S. (B0W 1R0).
Yarmouth Historical Society, 22 Collins St. Yarmouth, N.S. (B5A 3C8).

ANNAPOLIS VALLEY (Annapolis, Digby, Hants and Kings counties):
Admiral Digby Library and Historical Society, Box 863, Digby, N.S. (B0V 1A0).
Annapolis Valley Historical Society, Town Hall, Box 925, Middleton, N.S. (B0S 1P0).
Bear River Historical Society (Rev. E.F. Hall), Bear River, N.S. (B0S 1B0).
Hantsport & Area Historical Society, Box 525, Hantsport, N.S. (B0P 1P0).
Historical Association of Annapolis Royal, Box 68, Annapolis Royal, N.S. (B0S 1A0).

Kings Historical Society, Box 11, Kentville, N.S. (B4N 1S4).
Smith's Cove Historical Society, R.R. #1, Smith's Cove, N.S. (B0S 1S0) (M.J. Lawton, Secretary).
West Hants Historical Society, Box 177, Windsor, N.S. (B0N 2T0).

NORTHERN MAINLAND (Colchester and Cumberland counties):
Amherst Township Historical Society, 150 Church St., Amherst, N.S. (B4H 3C4).
Colchester Historical Society, Box 412, Truro, N.S. (B2N 5C5).
North Cumberland Historical Society, Box 52, Pugwash, N.S. (B0K 1L0).
Parrsboro Shore Historical Society, Box 98, Parrsboro, N.S. (B0M 1S0).
Tatamagouche Historical & Cultural Society, R.R. #1, Tatamagouche, N.S. (B0K 1V0) (Mr. Donald Hamilton).

OTHER:
The Black Cultural Society, 1016 Main St., Dartmouth, N.S. (B2W 4X9).
La Société Historique Acadienne, Box 2263, Sub-Station 'A,' Moncton, N.B. (E1C 8J3).
Millbrook Band Council, Box 634, Truro, N.S. (B2N 5E5).
Royal Nova Scotia Historical Society, Box 895, Armdale, N.S. (B3L 4K5).

Some of these groups have kindly given me an idea of their genealogical holdings. The **Beaton Institute of Cape Breton Studies** is open 8:30-4:30 (until 4:00 in summer), Monday to Friday. If you make prior arrangements, evening access can be given. Research may be done by yourself or by their staff within reason. They have church, cemetery, census, land, school, Bible records, passenger lists, some letters, journal and diaries, and some Cape Breton family trees. Address is Box 760, Sydney, N.S. (B1P 6J1).

Le **Centre d'Etudes Acadiennes,** Université de Moncton, Moncton, N.B. (E1A 3E9), is open weekdays 8:45-Noon, 1:00-4:30. It holds Acadian material for the Maritimes, including census, church and land records, available for your own research, as well as some passenger lists and newspapers; Private papers of Placide Gaudet, Auguste-E. Daigle, and Rev. Hector Hébert. As its major emphasis is genealogical, **Le Centre** is collecting and publishing such material, notably a proposed **Dictionnaire généalogique des familles acadiennes.** There is a guide to their holdings, **Inventaire général des Sources Documentaries sur les Acadiens,** the three volumes of which should assist anyone having an interest in Acadian genealogy. The genealogist is Stephen A. White, who provided much information about the Acadian material mentioned in this book.

The **Colchester Historical Society and Museum,** 29 Young St., Truro (B2N 3W3) collects material on Colchester County and the townships of Economy, Londonderry, Onslow and Truro, the town of Stewiacke, and other places in the county. Their outstanding record source is the cemeteries of the county, which are being typed and indexed for use. They also have local township books, school, land and census records. Hours in summer are 2-5 pm, except Mondays when they are closed. Wednesday, Friday and Sunday evenings they open from 7-9. In winter, they open Tuesday, Wednesday, Friday and Sunday only, from 2-5 pm, and on Friday evenings from 7-9 pm. Their maps and displays are very informative.

The **South Shore Genealogical Society** has rooms in Lunenburg Town Hall, and its postal address is Box 471, Bridgewater, N.S. B4V 2X6. This Society publishes a bi-monthly newsletter, and is publishing the cemetery inscriptions of Lunenburg, Queens and Shelburne Counties. Two volumes have appeared so far, and may be purchased from that Society for $17.50 each, postpaid.

Pictou County Historical Library and Archives is housed in the Thomas McCulloch House, Pictou. They have a number of letters and diaries in their growing manuscript collection. A number of indexed genealogies are on file and many are still in process of completion; both are available and of use. They are open from 15 May — 15 October, daily from 10am-5pm. You can make an appointment in the winter months, per Box 1210, Pictou, N.S. (B0K 1H0).

The **North Cumberland Historical Society,** R.R. #4, Pugwash, N.S. (B0K 1L0), has not a collection to be examined, but instead has adopted the policy of publishing its completed projects. Some of their publications deal with pioneers of Wallace Bay, the biographies of North Cumberlandians, the cemeteries of North Cumberland, churches and clergy of the area, and a history of Pugwash. The address given is that of Peter Vale, secretary of the society.

La Société Historique Acadienne de la Baie Ste.-Marie, Church Point, (B0W 1M0), directed by J.A. Deveau, is open 9am-4pm. You may do your own work by appointment, or pay $25.00 to have their staff examine records for you. If you do not read French or Latin, this service is reasonably priced. The library has land, school and church records, and passenger and voters lists, mostly to do with Acadians in western Nova Scotia.

At the other end of the·province, at Box 912, Sydney, the **Old Sydney Society** has premises open Monday to Friday, 8am-4:30pm. An appointment is recommended to see census, church, cemetery, land, private and probate records, as well as passenger lists. Mr. Eric Krause is the Assistant Historical Records Supervisor. Louisbourg and Isle-Royale records are held.

The New Glasgow branch, **Pictou-Antigonish Regional Library,** has 63 volumes of Pictou County cemeteries with an index volume, as well as the

1838 census for Pictou County (except Maxwelton), marriages 1825-1838, deaths 1864, 1866-1877, scrapbooks of clippings, indexes to Ross's **Pioneers and Churches,** and to Patterson's **History of Pictou County.** At the Hector Centre, Pictou, there is an extensive cross-referenced genealogy file. Another source of local information, including family history, is the Shell Collection, housed in the **Angus L. Macdonald Library,** St. Francis Xavier University, in Antigonish. A card index to **The Casket** newspaper is located here.

Last, but not least, is the **Yarmouth County Historical Society Museum,** 22 Collins St., Yarmouth, N.S. It is open every afternoon on weekdays throughout the year, but in the mornings as well in summer. They have local histories of Kemptville, Lake Annis, Pinckney's Point, Port Maitland-Beaver River, and Pubnico, and extensive Acadian material compiled by E.A. D'Entremont. There are family records of the names Butler, Churchill, Chute, H(e)aley, Hatfield, Kenney, Lent, Locke, Kelley, Nickerson, Porter, Rankin, Robbins, and Waitstill Lewis. A Loyalist collection includes the families of Andrews, Earl, Gavel, Hurlburt, Jeffrey, McKinnon, Raynard, Tooker and Van Norden. There is an index to the Crowell genealogy collection, and Clement Doane's county families and cemetery records. They have the original proprietors' book of Yarmouth, Town Point Cemetery, Hebron Baptist Church and Jeboque (Cheboque) Church records.

Publications

There are three publications that feature material of use to Nova Scotians doing family history. The oldest, founded in 1961, is the quarterly **Cahiers de la Société Historique Acadienne,** Box 2263, Sub-Staton 'A,' Moncton, N.B. Subscription is $7.50 a year. It has carried genealogies (e.g., Trahan), census and marriage records, a description of Le Centre D'Etudes Acadiennes in Moncton, and an important article in English, "Major Sources for Acadian Genealogical Research" (**Cahier** 29).

The Nova Scotia Historical Review, available for $7.50 a year from 6016 University Avenue, Halifax, N.S. B3H 1W4, has succeeded the former **Nova Scotia Historical Quarterly.** It has continued the policy of publishing a genealogy in each issue, recently augmenting the family tree with an historical background for the family.

Genealogical Association of Nova Scotia

The Royal Nova Scotia Historical Society had a genealogical committee during the 1970's. In 1982 this was disbanded and replaced by a Genealogical Association, under the chairmanship of the author. The Association is a group of volunteers who put out a genealogical magazine, **The Nova Scotia Genealogist,** occasional publications (see section about newspapers), and hold workshops. The magazine appears three times a year and membership in the Association costs $10.00 per year (1983). The magazine publishes members' queries and replies, family Bible records, book reviews, a bulletin board of news, and articles of interest. Members may publish queries at $1.00 apiece, while non-members pay $2.00 each. Issues of the former **Newsletter** (21 and 33) are indexes to the series, while any back issues can be ordered from the Publications Secretary, Box 895, Armdale, N.S. B3L 4K5. Prices on request, with stamped self-addressed envelope, Subscriptions/membership may be sent to the Membership Secretary, Box 641, Station M. Halifax, N.S. B3J 2T3.

You should understand, however, that the Genealogical Association has no library nor does research for hire. Its concerns are its publications programme, query exchanges, workshops, and the standard of genealogical practice in Nova Scotia.

Registrar General of Nova Scotia

In the chapter on the Public Archives of Nova Scotia, R.G.32 was described in some detail. The subsequent records of birth, marriage, and death in Nova Scotia are held in the files of the Registrar General of Nova Scotia. Civil registration began in the province on 1 October 1908, and virtually every vital statistic since then is recorded by this office, whose address is Deputy Registrar General, Box 157, Halifax, N.S. (B3J 2M9). The public may not examine the actual records, but the department will attempt to help those who provide full information and send in the appropriate fees.

The Registrar must be advised of the full name of the person born, married, or deceased; the date and place of the event; the names of the parents of anyone for whom a birth certificate is required; and you must state why you want the certificate. If the document is needed for the preparation of a genealogy, that reason should be stated. The fee is $5.00 for a short form certificate, and $10.00 for a long form. If you do not know the exact date the Registrar will make a search through 3 years (the year you mention and the adjacent year on either side) for $2.00. If the entry is found this $2.00 is included in the certificate fee. If the record is not found, your search fee will be kept in payment. Cause of death will not be revealed on death certificates, I am told. If you wish to telephone, the number is 1-902-424-4374.

By now, you will have been through the most likely avenues of information about your Nova Scotia ancestry: family circle, secondary printed matter, the Public Archives of Nova Scotia, sundry provincial offices and societies, and perhaps taken out a few subscriptions. There is one last source of assistance before you can put everything you have found together. You may wish to find your pre-Nova Scotian ancestry, and to write to an out-of-province record repository. But eventually you will reach the plateau at which progress stops or slows down appreciably. Then, you might like to talk things over with a genealogist of experience in such matters.

I shall not dwell long upon the genealogist of experience, except to say that he or she will generally be a person who has learned by years of trial and error to see paths of approach that are unnoticed by others. Such a person often has gained what I can only call "a feel" for genealogical research and for families. You will not find a miracle worker, but you will be in touch with someone who — ideally — has something of value to your quest. Shall I tell you to be patient: yours is not the only genealogy they have ever seen or are working on, and they may be very busy. Then you must be prepared to wait or go to someone else. Will you seek a guaranteed result, because anyone who promises to find something without thorough investigation may be just posing as a genealogist. You should expect to pay for the time and the experience of a real genealogist. Most such people in Nova Scotia do not do it for a living, so they are subsidizing those they help by working cheaply. But they do expect and deserve remuneration in most instances. Such people have every right to refuse an offer to do research for you or me or anyone else. Some potential clients come across as cheapskates who want everything right away, and offer no solid clues upon which work can commence. Is it surprising that such a customer gets no one who is willing to work for them? So, prepare first, be reasonable and patient, and your chances will be better. And remember, if you agree to pay someone so much an hour to "look for your family tree" and they don't find it, you still owe them for the time. If you promise to pay me $5.00 an hour to catch trout for you, the most I can do is offer the fish bait in the likeliest places. I cannot guarantee a catch, only the attempt to catch. Most researchers have got stung once or twice by clients who wouldn't pay because nothing was found. As a result, many genealogists ask for payment of a retainer in advance.

Experienced genealogists know about many things that the general public either do not know about, or would not have thought of as sources of help with their family tree. Some genealogists have compiled their own finding aids and indexes over the years, on their own time and by their own efforts. They may have colleagues that they swap help with on the basis of these private files. Some genealogists know funeral directors with good death records from pre-1908, and can find information that is not otherwise obtainable. Sometimes, an experienced hand can pinpoint names with amazing geographical accuracy just by having a long memory for surnames they have run across. The genealogist will know that sometimes you can't get any further here with a family, but that a brother of your ancestor moved to the United States and died there. Both American naturalization and death records are older and better than the Nova Scotian ones, and often state parentage of the newcomer or the deceased. The father of that brother is the father of the ancestor who stayed here, and the family tree moves on again. Therefore, it is often foolish to ignore the advice of an experienced person.

A Genealogical Profession

The demand for hired researchers has called forth a response from people whose abilities range from the expert through the competent to the downright incapable. Few Maritimers have seriously considered making a living as genealogical researchers, partly due to lack of clientele, and partly due to a lack of accreditation to do such research.

What happens is that someone traces his family for several generations and has not submitted his work to critical analysis or for publication. He may wish to do research for others. Such work may be excellent, or it may not be. Quality must be a major concern once one works for hire as a researcher.

The Conference of New England Governors/Eastern Canadian Premiers has recommended that genealogy be recognized as a bona fide profession. The constitution of the Genealogical Association of Nova Scotia favours the setting of standards of genealogical research. The Genealogical Institute of the Maritimes (Centre of Acadian Studies, University of Moncton, Moncton, N.B. E1A 3E9) undertakes to supply lists of qualified genealogical practitioners in the region.

Meanwhile there are a few things you should bear in mind if you hire a researcher. Read Brenda Merriam's article, "Wanted: Hired Genealogist" in **Canadian Genealogist**, 3, 4 (1981), and Lois Kernaghan's "Hired Genealogist: an addendum with some further pointers," in the same, 4, 1 (1982). You may obtain these for $5.00 each from George Hancocks, 172 King Henry's Blvd., Agincourt, Ontario M1T 2V6, or subscribe to this very important publication for $20.00 a year.

V — GETTING IT TOGETHER: ARRANGEMENT AND PRESENTATION OF RESULTS

After you have collected your genealogical information and arranged it into a tentative family tree, you will have to decide what you want to do with it. Unless you are a **bonave** (Irish for 'a little pig'), you will not hoard your findings and risk their loss or destruction. You will want to share your findings, either to the world at large by publicaton, or to your relations by private circulation of copies of your results.

Many of you will have valuable, possibly unique, genealogical information. There is consequently much that stands to be lost forever unless it is recorded somewhere. There are a number of approaches to the arrangement of genealogical information. You can draw a chart or write a family history of sorts. You can choose a progenitor or ancestor and trace all of his descendants in a male line, or ALL of his descendants; or you can trace simply your own direct line of descent.

Whatever method you choose, you need a logical method of recording your findings. Card-indexing, recording on looseleaf pages, preparing printed charts, are all good enough, as far as they go. They do encourage a sort of myopia, however, by putting too much emphasis on a name and date approach. These are good recording methods, but there will come the day when you will want to sit down and prepare a completed family history either for publication or as a permanent record for your family members.

Then, you will require a format that is both understandable to you and your readers, and in keeping with generally accepted genealogical practice. I suggest that you should sift your evidence thoroughly before beginnng a written or narrative family history. That way, you avoid several failings common to too many genealogical compilations: impossible births, unexplained abbreviations, eccentric presentation of facts, repetition, lack of precision, afterthoughts, etc. What we shall do, then, before going into some explanation of the two commonest and (I believe) best formats in use today

107

for family history, is to examine some methods of ironing out bugs from the family tree data, and to offer a list of abbreviations that have been used or may be used in genealogy.

Checking Your Results

You can make two arrangements of your material and see how well they cross-check. Line up your results chronologically, then by name and place. Review it carefully, and you may find births of children within nine months of one another, and women having a child born when they were past 50, and deaths of people appearing to be aged over 100. You can safely assume that in the days before incubators, women did not generally bear two children within nine months of one another. I once reviewed a manuscript genealogy which gave a child born 18 June 1856, another 2 Dec. 1856, and yet another 19 Aug. 1857. The author should have caught this, but didn't. Examination of the manuscript revealed that the 2 Dec. 1856 birth belonged to the family of the brother of the man being given as the child's father, in good probability, since both families had a child, Wesley Albert, and in the brother's family this child was given as "born about 1855-1858," while in the family under discussion, the 1871 census showed a "W.A., male, age 12."

People in past generations loved to exaggerate the age of their elderly relatives, and this creates something of a bugbear to the modern genealogist. It may go against the grain to accept that some grandparent who attended meeting every Sunday, read his Bible daily, and was honest in all of his dealings, would nevertheless claim without batting an eye to be five or even ten years older than he really was. In consequence, when such a one died, the family had his declared age carved on the headstone. Nova Scotian cemeteries abound in stones to those aged beyond reasonable probability. Yes, some of our ancestors lived to the century, but probably far fewer than we think. In eighty cases of death ages above 90 which I have been able to check (another seventy I could not obtain authentic birth records), I have found that fifty-two were accurate within one year, twenty were exaggerated two to ten years (and one by twelve years), and eight were underestimated by two to four years. In every one of the eight underestimated ages, what happened was "'rounding off'' — e.g., a man aged 93 was recorded as aged 90, or 97 as 95.

Women bearing children beyond the age of fifty must be regarded as very exceptional. I suppose that a few rare cases exist, but they are few enough to be dismissed from our serious consideration. You may as well recognize that something like 99% of births to women past their mid-forties are recorded mistakenly or falsely. In many instances, the family historian

has copied or muddled the dates and ages. These can be resolved by checking over your information in just such a chronological arrangement as we
are now discussing. But, what of a record that states by inference that a
woman of fifty-one is the mother of a newborn infant? If there is a space
between the birth of her last child and that of this child, you may investigate
to see if the man lost his former wife and had remarried another having the
same or similar Christian name. If it is clear that his wife was still alive and
well, you must consider if there could have been another couple of similar
name in the community, who might have begot the child. Also consider if
the primary record could be mixed up: did the minister write down the
baptism from memory a week later, and confuse the godparents' names with
those of the physical parents? One final consideration must be that sometimes the teenaged daughter of a women of fifty would bear an illigitimate
child whom the grandparents hoped to pass of as a belated addition to their
own family.

Secondly, arrange your material by order of names. Careful combing of
the evidence this way should eliminate irritating duplications, and prevent
what I call afterthought genealogy — the type where, after the family groups
have been worked out, snippets of overlooked information about the various
members get tacked on. This can be really worse than leaving out the additional information if it serves to confuse the reader, or to raise questions
about the original evidence. One example from my own experience will show
what I mean. Charles X was written up with four children, named and
worked out. Three pages later, the compiler tacked on Charles X's will, with
its bequests to his "five children." Since Charles X lived to be about 80, and
had been a widower for thirty-two years, the fifth child must have grown up.
What became of him? The author, when questioned, said something along
the lines of, "Oh yeah, that was mum's Uncle Bill. Didn't I put him in?"
Better that he should have checked his work than that someone else should
have caught the error. You can well imagine that my confidence in the remainder of that author's facts was rather diminished.

Another problem, often met with, that alphabetical sorting should min-
imize, is that of the "left over" people. The compiler finds he can fit in most
of the people of a name in the area, and then comes up with a half dozen
strays. Careful cross-checking will reveal that at least some odds and ends of
data can be fitted into the details of some accountable individuals. And
sometimes, you get left with strays who cannot belong, do not belong but
yet defy all attempts to explain them away. Such a one was Augustine Punch
of Antigonish County in an 1838 church record. He must be an error in the
original record, but any presentation of that family ought to have an appendix or footnotes or something of the kind to which these unaccounted people can be relegated. The reader has a right to know that such individuals

109

existed or seemed to exist. There is nothing to forbid inclusion in your genealogy of statements such as, "This John McKay may be identical with John
McKay of the brig 'Thalia,' which made a voyage to the northern Pacific
during the years 1856-58." You are not saying that it was the same name,
but you are drawing attention to a fact about a man of the name in the
community who made such a voyage. Among his descendants, someone
may recall having heard that their greatgrandfather has "sailed around the
world," which may fill out the sense of what sort of man their ancestor had
been.

Abbreviations

This is presented as a means of helping you to use published genealogies and to present your own family tree in chart or narrative form. Many
abbreviations are common to other fields beside genealogy and where an
abbreviation will be likely to be found in any dictionary list, it has been
omitted. The following is a list of some of those more specific to genealogy
and which do not always gain inclusion in general lists.

Admon. — Administration (of an estate)

ae., aet. — **aetatis** (Latin) "of age" — e.g., d.15 May 1829, ae. 29 years (29
years of age).

b. — born, birth (symbolized *).

bap., bapt. — baptized, baptism (symbolized ~)

bur. — buried, burial (symbolized ▢).

c., ca. — **circa** (Latin) "about" — e.g., aged ca. 80 years.

ch. — child, children

conf. — confirmed, confirmation

d. — died, death (symbolized +). .

dau. — daughter.

desc. — descendants.

doc. — document.

d.s.p. — **decessit sine proele** (Latin) — died without issue.

d.s.p.l. — **decessit sine proele legitime** (Latin) — died without lawful issue.

d.s.p.m. — **decessit sine proele masculine** (Latin) — died without male issue.

d.v.m. — **decessit vita matris** (Latin) — died in mother's lifetime.

d.v.p. — **decessit vita patris** (Latin) — died in father's lifetime.

d.y. — died young; the inference is that the child died before the age of
majority — i.e., 21.

et al. — **et alii** (Latin) — and others.

et ux. — **et uxor** (Latin) — and wife.

f. — **folio** (Latin) — page (on deeds).

gd. — granddaughter.

gs. — grandson
lib. — **liber** (Latin) — book (on deeds).
m. — married, marriage (symbolized = or ∞).
m. (2) — married secondly.
M.G. — Manuscripts Group.
M.I. — Monumental Inscription (what the tombstones say).
M.L.B. — Marriage License Bond.
n.d. — no date.
n.f.r. — no further record.
N.S. — New Style (date by Gregorian reckoning).
ob., obit. — **obiit** (Latin) — died.
O.S. — Old Style (dates by Julian reckoning).
P.A.N.S. — Public Archives of Nova Scotia.
pr. — proved (of will).
res. — resided, residence (sometimes r.).
R.G. — Record Group.
twp. — township.
unm. — unmarried
viv. — **vivens** (Latin) — living.
wid. — widow.
widr., wdwr. — widower.
+ — died.
= — married.
↓ — had children.

Methods of Presentation

When you have arranged and checked over your material, put in the proper abbreviations, and decided to consider a good arrangement for your findings, the best step you can take is to put your family tree on a chart. This may take several sheets of paper, joined together, but when you have sketched out the "shape" of the family tree, you will not only see how it fits together, but perhaps gain some insight into the best way of presenting it in narrative form.

The two most generally accepted formats for presentation of narrative genealogy are the Burke method and the New England method. The former is named after the publisher in Great Britain, Burke's Peerage Limited, who developed it. A good brief explanation of the system may be found in the introductory pages of **Burke's Irish Family Records.** It is well suited to families in which large numbers of male lines do not require to be traced. It is the better method if your purpose is to follow the lineage of heads of families.

The latter format takes its name from the **New England Historical and Genealogical Register**. Gilbert H. Doane, in chapter 11 of his book **Searching For Your Ancestors**, offers a useful guide to this style of presentation. The New England method is very serviceable for presentation of large families in which numerous family groups are to be treated. So that you may see how the two methods compare to each other and to a genealogical chart, the following family tree is recorded on a chart. Then we show two pedigrees, one in the Burke, the other in the New England method.

Chart

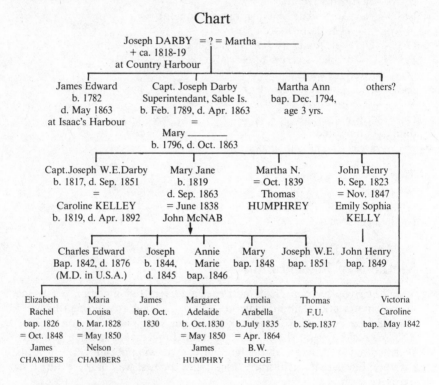

BURKE METHOD

Lawrence POWER and his wife, Catherine POWER, both of Kilmacthomas, Co. Waterford, Ireland, had issue including:
1. Catherine, b. 1795, d. 11 Aug. 1864; = (1) 11 May 1818, Philip (1787-1827), son of Thomas RYAN of Co. Kilkenny, and had issue. Catherine = (2) 25 Oct. 1834, Thomas (1806-1862), son of Patrick RING of Ballyragget, Co. Kilkenny, and had issue.

2. Eleanor, b. 1800, d. 25 Feb. 1866; = (1) 19 Sep. 1819, Daniel BUCKLEY, grocer (1784-1839) from Co. Cork, and had issue. Eleanor = (2) 16 July 1840, Peter MORRISSEY, brewer (1788-1868) from Co. Kilkenny.
3. Bridget, b. 1801, d. 9 Oct. 1861; = 9 Feb. 1822, Michael, son of Michael HIGGINS of Co. Londonderry, Ireland, and had issue.
4. Mary, b. 1804, d. 3 Sep. 1877; = 3 Sep. 1824, John HOWLETT of Co. Wexford. Issue.
5. Margaret, b. 1809; = (1) 5 June 1830, William (b. 1802), son of James MURPHY of Halifax, and had issue. Margaret = (2) _____ QUINN.
6. Anne, b. 1812, bur. 7 Mar. 1829 at Halifax.
7. Patrick Power, merchant and M.P., b. 17 Mar. 1815 at Kilmacthomas, d. 23 Feb. 1881 at Halifax; = 10 Oct. 1840, Ellen (1815-1891), dau. of John GAUL. They had issue:
   (1) Lawrence Geoffrey Power, barrister, M.P., and Senator, b. 9 Aug. 1841 at Halifax, d. 12 Sep. 1921; = 23 June 1880, Susan (1860-1926), dau. of Michael O'LEARY of West Quoddy, N.S. They had issue:
   (1a) Mary E., Sister Maura of the Sisters of Charity of Halifax, b. 24 May 1881, d. 16 Jan. 1957.
   (2a) Patrick, b. 12 Mar. 1883, d. 21 Feb. 1889.
   (3a) Catherine, b. 13 Jan. 1885, d. 1961, unm.
   (2) John, twin, b. 14 Apr. 1843, d. 15 Apr. 1843.
   (3) Catherine, twin, a nun, b. 14 Apr. 1843, d. 12 Apr. 1871 at Manhattanville, New York.
   (4) Mary, b. 26 Dec. 1846; = 30 Nov. 1882, Judge Angus McISAAC (b. 1844) of Antigonish. They had five children, only one of whom, Mrs. BOYD, left issue.
   (5) Patrick David, b. 3 Aug. 1848, lost on S.S. "City of Boston" in Jan. 1870, unm.
   (6) Edmund, b. 1850, d. 7 Apr. 1866, age 15 yr. 6 mos.
   (7) David Lullus, b. Oct. 1852, d. 2 May 1856.
   (8) Ellen Clothilde, b. June 1855, d. 18 Aug. 1894, a Sacred Heart nun.

Note that there are four generations shown on the above: the progenitor (Lawrence); his seven children, each designated by an Arabic number; the eight grandchildren, each indicated by an Arabic number within parentheses (1), (2), etc.; and the fourth generation is indicated by an Arabic number and the letter **a**. A fifth generation would substitute **b** as the letter, the sixth generation **c**, and so forth. Each generation is indented to the right of the one before it. The family tree unfolds in its entirety as you go along. All names under a person, and which are indented further to the right of him or her, are the offspring and descendants of that person.

NEW ENGLAND METHOD

1. Isaac RIGBY, carpenter, d. 3 Jan. 1826, age 62; = 13 July 1791 = Rachel, d. 4 Feb. 1850, age 77 at North Sydney, dau. of Samuel RUDOLPH of Halifax, and had issue:

    1. Samuel, bap. 29 June 1793, viv. 1825.

2.   2. John. bap. 12 July 1795, viv. 1825.

3.   3. Isaac, bap. 23 Aug. 1798, d. 5 Jan. 1887.

    4. Christiana Elizabeth, bap. 10 May 1801. d. 6 Dec. 1802.

    5. George Thomas, bap 22 May 1803, d. 24 Aug. 1803.

    6. Edward, bap. 19 May 1805, viv. 1825.

4.   7. Charles Henry, bap. 31 May 1807, d. 4 Jan. 1866.

    8. George, bap. 28 May 1809, viv. 1825.

    9. Prevost Frederick, bap. 19 May 1811, viv. 1825.

5.   10. Douglas Gordon, b. 1813, viv. 1871.

    11. Thomas, b. 16 Feb. 1815, viv. 1825.

  2. John Rigby^2 (Isaac^1), carpenter, bap. 12 July 1795, viv. 1825; = Mary _____ and had issue:

    1. a child.

    2. Mary Anne, "2nd child," b. 22 June 1819.

  3. Isaac Rigby^2 (Isaac^1), gardener, bap. 23 Aug. 1798, d. 5 Jan. 1887; = c. 1822 = Elizabeth, d. 14 Sep. 1867, age 70, dau. of Edmund WARD. She died at Kentville, he at Halifax. Issue:

    1. Elizabeth Dorothy, b. 29 Aug. 1823 = 24 Oct. 1850 = Howard D. STEELE, barrister.

    2. Rachel Frances, bap. 23 June 1825.

    3. Mary, b. 1 Apr, 1827, d.9. Dec. 1837.

    4. Hannah Ward, b. 17 May 1829, d. 5 Oct. 1842.

    5. Eleanor Mundell, b. 4 Aug. 1831.

    6. Henrietta Phillips, b. 14 Feb. 1834.

    7. Emily, b. 11 Nov. 1837.

    8. Mary Caroline, twin, b. 5 July 1839.

6.   9. Charles Douglas, twin, b. 5 July 1839, d. 17 Feb. 1888.

    10. Edward Albert, bap. 17 July 1842.

  4. Charles Henry Rigby^2 (Isaac^1), Customs Officer at Glace Bay, bap. 31 May 1807, d. 4 Jan. 1866 at Sydney; = (1) 25 May 1828, Frances Wentworth, dau. of Edmund WARD, and had issue:

    1. Charles Isaac, b. 20 Apr. 1829, d. 13 Jan. 1830.

    2. William Henry, b. 13 May 1831, viv. 1844.

  Charles Henry Rigby = (2) 22 Aug. 1829, Mary Anne DRISCOLL, and had further issue:

    3. Sarah Ann, b. 21 May 1841.

    4. Charles, b. 8 Oct. 1843.

    5. Catherine Sarah, b. 31 Oct. 1845.

6. James Isaac, b. 26 Jan. 1848, bur. 16 Apr. 1852.
  5. Douglas Gordon Rigby[2] (Isaac[1]), accountant; = Mary Caroline
    CLARKE, who d. at Sydney Mines, 6 Nov. 1867, age 53. They
    had a son,
7.   1. Samuel Gordon, b. 1842, d. 18 July 1886.
  6. Charles Douglas Rigby, M.D.[3] (Isaac[2], Isaac[1]), b. 5 July 1839, twin, d.
    17 Feb. 1888; = Mate Louise GIBBS, viv. 1903, and had issue:
    1. Charles Edward Stuart, b. 7 Nov. 1872.
    2. Emily Mary, b. 18 May 1874.
    3. Gertrude Henrietta, b. 16 Feb. 1876.
  7. Samuel Gordon Rigby[3] (Douglas G.[2], Isaac[1]), judge, b. 1842, d. 18
    July 1886; - 2 June 1874 = Elizabeth Archibald (1851-16 Nov.
    1936), dau. of Charles BURNYEAT, Dartmouth. Issue:
    1. Charles Gordon, b. 9 Apr. 1877.
    2. Edwin Douglas, b. 17 May 1878.
    3. Mary Kathleen, b. 1880.
    4. Elizabeth Alice, b. 11 Feb. 1882.
    5. Kathleen, b. 6 Dec. 1884.

Whenever a male had a family that is traced further, this method indicates the fact by sequential numbers in the left hand margins. Each family
group is headed by the father with his generation number and ancestry to
the progenitor.

· · · · · · · · · · · ·

You must decide which method will best convey the fruits of your genealogical labours. Whichever format you select, be sure that you adhere to
it and do not leap back and forth between the two. Without years of hard
experience, do not attempt to devise your method for any published genealogy. People can make up a shorthand of their own that is so arcane that no
one can decipher it; John S. Thompson and his son, the future prime minister, had a system of notation that was so unique that it was not cracked for
a century.

Once you complete your family tree you should write your family history. It will be more interesting to the reader than the tree itself. A family
history sets out in an attractive fashion the story from your earliest ancestor.
It should also include the wider historical background of the family. What
conditions in the old country made them leave? What were matters like
when they reached Nova Scotia?

Getting Behind It

People do not exist in a vacuum. There can be no doubt that your genealogical work is incomplete when you have arranged your names and dates in keeping with some sequence. You must investigate the history of the places in which your family lived. A pedigree full of names and dates is fine, if you like skeletons! How about putting flesh on the bare bones? Shall these bones live, or shall they languish as the pallid remains of human beings who lived and worked, breathed and loved?

Earlier we provided a list of community and county histories. Unfortunately, there is no modern history of the whole province written for adults. In **The Atlantic Provinces** (1967), William E. Morley lists local histories written before 1950. In the bibliography to **The Atlantic Provinces . . . 1712-1857,** W.S. MacNutt cites some books and articles written to 1972. Robert Vaison, **Nova Scotia Past and Present** (1976) takes the bibliography almost to date. My advice is that you try to get material on the country and community where your forebears lived, then move into the aspects of the general history of Nova Scotia that have been written up. My series in **Bluenose Magazine** supplies some notion of the ethnic groups and their coming into Nova Scotia, and provides a bibliography for each of the eight major groups. There are five particularly interesting articles on Nova Scotia historical demography (population studies) that may help to supply you with background information about your ancestry and the province of various periods. These are:

Bird, J. Brian, "Settlement Patterns in Maritime Canada," **The Geographical Review,** XLV, part 3 (1955), pp. 385-404.

Hobson, Peggie M., "Population and Settlement in Nova Scotia," **The Scottish Geographical Magazine,** LXX, No. 2 (1954), pp. 49-63.

MacLean, M.C., "The Mobile Nova Scotian," **Public Affairs,** II, No. 1 (Aug. 1938), pp. 6-9.

Martell, James S., "The Mingling of Nationalities in Nova Scotia," **Journal of Education,** VII, No. 1 (Jan., 1936), pp. 70-73.

Millward, Hugh, **Regional Patterns of Ethnicity in Nova Scotia: a Geographical Study,** 58 pp. (Ethnic Heritage Series, VI)

Very useful is the Ethnic Heritage Series published by the International Education Centre, Saint Mary's University, Halifax, N.S. B3H 3C3. Contact the Centre for a list of publications and prices.

. . . .

Commonest Names in the Counties

This section offers two important pieces of information about each county in Nova Scotia. In order, we shall look at each county in 1881 and see its population then, and accompany this with a ranking of the seven largest ethnic groups in each. Then we shall provide a list of the ten most commonly occurring surnames in the 1870-71 directory.

Annapolis County (20,598 people) was English (57%), Irish (13%), Scottish (10%), German (10%), African (4%), French (2%), Indian (0.3%). The most common surnames were Harris (36), Brown (35), Chute (32), Parker (30), Banks (29), Morse (27), Potter (27), Whitman (27), Phinney (26), and Marshall (25).

Antigonish County (18,060 people) was Scottish (68.5%), French (16%), Irish (9%), English (3%), German (2%), African (0.3%), Indian (0.1%). The most frequest surnames were McDonald (160), Chisholm (90), McGillivray (71), McPherson (27), Fraser (25), Gillis (24), Cameron (22), McKinnon (20), Grant (18), McIsaac (18), and Smith (18).

Cape Breton County (31,258 people). Origins were Scottish (65.3%), English (15%), Irish (13%), French (4%), German (0.9%), Indian (0.8%), African (0.1%). The ten most common surnames were McDonald (97), McLean (30), Gillis (26), McIntyre (25), McKinnon (21), McLeod (20), Campbell (16), McInnis (14), Hill (12), and Morrison (12).

Colchester County (26,720 people) was Scottish (38.1%), Irish (32.4%), English (20.5%), German (4%), French (1.5%), African (0.7%), Indian (0.3%). Leading names were Fulton (42), McKay (34), Archibald (33), Sutherland (31), Crowe (29), Creelman (25), Johnson (23), Davison (23), Smith (22), and Fisher (21).

Cumberland County (27,368 people) was English (54.3%), Scottish (19.4%), Irish (17.2%), French (3.8%), German (1.9%), African (0.6%, Indian (0.4%). Most numerous names were Smith (35), Purdy (18), Black (17), Bent (16), Mills (16), Stevens (16), Embree (14), Harrison (14), Angevine (13), Brown (13), Logan (13), and Noiles (13).

Digby County's population in 1881 was 19,881, of whom the ethnic origins were English (45.5%), French (39.7%), Irish (5%), African (2.5%), Scottish (2.5%), German (2.5%), and Indian (0.7%). The major surnames were Rice (28), Melanson (27), Amirault (26), Jones (22), Comeau (19), Gaudet (17), Marshall (17), Outhouse (17), LeBlanc (16), and McNeil (16).

Guysborough County had 17,808 people. In origin, they were Scottish (30.3%), English (25.1%), Irish (22.3%), German (7.8%), French (7.7%), African (5.1%), and Indian (0.5%). Numerous names included McDonald (42), Chisholm (20), McKean (20), Cameron (19), Carr (18), Archibald (16), Smith (16), Hadley (15), McKenzie (13), and McLean (13).

117

Halifax City has 36,100 people, of whom the origins were Irish (35.5%), English (32.4%), Scottish (18.1%), German (6%), African (3%), French (2.6%), and Indian (almost nil). Most common surnames were Smith (82), Murphy (72), McDonald (60), Power (60), Walsh (60), Brown (48), O'Brien (43), Fraser (42), Wilson (41), and Kennedy (40).

Halifax County had 31,817 people, whose origins were English (24%), Irish (21.1%), German (19%), Scottish (18%), French (9.2%), African (4.7%), and Indian (0.2%). The ten leading surnames were Smith (49), Boutlier (31), Conrad (29), Gaetz (28), Murphy (26), Moser (25), Slaunwhite (23), Hubley (21), Thomas (21), and McDonald (20).

Hants County, with 23,359 people, was English (39.3%), Scottish (25.1%), Irish (24.2%), German (6.4%), French (1.3%), African (1%), and Indian (0.4%). Most common county names were Smith (89), Harvie (46), Mosher (34), Dimock (29), McDonald (27), Sanford (26), Parker (24), Densmore (23), Cochran (21), and O'Brien (21).

Inverness County's 25,651 people were Scottish (75.1%), French (14.2%), English (5.1%), Irish (5%), Indian (0.4%), German and African (almost nil). The leading names were all Scottish: McDonald (222), McLean (98), Campbell (74), McKinnon (72), Gillis (65), Cameron (61), McEachern (61), McLellan (50), McDougal (44), and McKay (43).

Kings County, with 23,469 people, was English (63.2%), Irish (17.9%), Scottish (9.5%), German (4.7%), French (2.1%), African (1.3%), and Indian (0.4%). The most numerous names were Newcomb (37), Eaton (33), Bishop (31), Borden (31), Harris (25), Caldwell (21), Ells (19), Ward (19), and Davidson (21).

Lunenburg County's 28,583 people were German (70.7%), English (13.9%), French (6.6%), Scottish (3.9%), Irish (3.3%), Indian (0.2%), and African (0.1%). Leading surnames were Eisenhauer (34), Zinck (33), Wentzel (31), Rafuse (30), Hebb (25), Keddy (25), Conrad (21), Hiltz (21), Lohnes (21), Wile (21), Young (21), and Zwicker (21).

Pictou County, with 35,535 people, was heavily Scottish (82.8%), with a few English (6.4%), Irish (6.1%), German (2.5%), French (0.8%), Indian (0.5%), and African (0.3%). The ten most plentiful names were of Scottish origin: Fraser (226), McDonald (213), McKenzie (135), McKay (88), Cameron (85), Grant (77), Sutherland (68), McLeod (64), Ross (61), and Murray (60).

Queens County's 10,577 people made it the least populous county in Nova Scotia in 1881. The ethnic background of its people included English (42.7%), German (24.5%), Scottish (12.5%), Irish (10.6%), African (3.3%), French (2.6%), and Indian (0.9%). The most numerous surnames a century ago were Freeman (52), Smith (31), Kempton (25), Gardner (23), McLeod (20), Minard (18), Harlow (17), Dexter (16), Ford (16), and Leslie (16).

Richmond County, with 15,121 people, was the only county in which the French were the leading ethnic group (48.6%), followed by the Scottish (35.7%), Irish (8.1%), English (5.9%), Indian (0.7%), German (0.2%), and African (0.1%). Major names were Boudreau (60), LeBlanc (40), Landry (34), Morrison (25), Fougère (21), Sampson (19), Forrest (17), Poirier (15), Marchand (14), and Vigneault (11).

Shelburne County's 14,913 people were English (62.1%), Scottish (13.6%), German (9.1%), Irish (8.5%), African (3%), French (1.2%), and Indian (0.3%). Most numerous names were Nickerson (92), Smith (81), Crowell (59), Perry (56), Swaine (36), Snow (31), Bower (23), Doane (23), Hopkins (22), and Hardy (21).

Victoria County, with 12,470 people, was the most Scottish county (83.2%), with English (8.3%), a distant second. Other groups included Irish (5.7%), French (0.9%), Indian (0.7%), and German (0.1%). All the most numerous surnames were Scottish: McDonald (46), McLeod (37), McKenzie (32), McRae (32), McNeil (21), Campbell (20), McLean (20), Morrison (19), McKay (17), and McAulay (15).

Yarmouth County in 1881 had 21,284 people. By origin, there were English (53.9%), French (35.2%), Irish (5.3%), Scottish (2.4%), African (1.4%) German (1.1%), and Indian (0.2%). Most numerous surnames were Crosby (55), D'Entremont (50), Allen (48), Porter (37), Durkee (34), Amirault (33), Hatfield (31), Hurlburt (28), Surette (28), and Killam (26).

Naturally, these are but a selection of the surnames in the several counties of Nova Scotia; and a complete list of family names would be a volume in itself. In most counties the ten most common surnames taken together do not account for above one-sixth of the total population of their county. However, the less common names tend to be much more easily localized by researchers, so that rare surnames such as Estey (Halifax), Batton (Annapolis), and Eadie (Antigonish) are generally more quickly pinned down geographically than are some of the more widespread surnames. Imagine the difficulty you would have if you sought a MacDonald or a Fraser from Nova Scotia, and had not an inkling as to which county they came from. By comparison, finding the area where the Publicovers or the Ettingers lived is easy, though neither name is exactly to be regarded as scarce in Nova Scotia today. But a century ago, the Publicovers frequented Lunenburg County and the Ettingers were only to be found in Hants County.

Directories can be misleading, as they tended to list the more prominent people or those who lived in the more important settled areas. In Richmond County, for example, the name Martel was in 1871 the sixth most common surname, and Mombourquette the ninth, yet neither appears prominently in the directory of 1870-71.

Knowledge of these and other pieces of background information will greatly assist your research in Nova Scotia. For it is really only when you get behind the facts and figures, the names and dates, of your particular family tree that you can begin to see your ancestry in the perspective of the community and the province.

Giving Something Back

So far, we have placed the emphasis on getting things, because human nature being what it is, we generally take more interest in gaining than in giving. But I hope that as you read through these pages you may have sensed that my philosophy of genealogy favours giving as well as getting. If you think about the matter for a few minutes, you will perceive that the generosity of giving is nothing more than enlightened self-interest.

Why should you or I spend time and money and then give away all or most of the results? Here are four replies to that question, which taken together, convince me that we ought to be forthcoming with our assistance when it is possible within some degree of reason. Firstly, as the years pass there is an inevitable attrition; records do get lost or destroyed. By sharing information you help to preserve it from going the way of many records in past decades. Secondly, regard giving help as casting of bread upon the waters. Those who give help and act obliging and friendly tend to get more assistance from colleagues than do those crabbed, peevish individuals who hoard their few meagre scraps of information. I always think that it is only the man with one idea in his head that needs to fear giving his idea away. Thirdly, there is the kindness that those with more money or brains or luck owe to those others whose lot is not so fortunate in this world. Finally, sharing information can prevent much time and trouble being wasted on duplication of effort. If a job has been done well, why not put the money and effort into doing something else? There is ample scope for new research without someone covering the same ground twice.

What are some specific examples of giving help in genealogy? You can let others know the names and addresses of helpful and reliable agencies and individuals. Let people know through the **Nova Scotia Genealogist** what you are working on, and perhaps you will find someone else who is working on the same lineage and is willing to swap information. If you have or can borrow an old register or papers, take them to the P.A.N.S. for microfilming or photocopying, or deposit them there. If you are near the cemetery that has not been previously copied, why not copy it and put the results on file by making three copies; one for you, one for P.A.N.S., and one for the local historical society or the church congregation that has the cemetery. Issue No. 10 of the **Nova Scotia Genealogist** gives a suggested method of tombstone copying. The Nova Scotia Museum has Debbie Trask, who is an experienced tombstone investigator, and she has published several guides and commentaries on work in cemeteries from the historical viewpoint. If you do not feel like going alone into the graveyard, see if the nearest historical society is interested. Perhaps if you can get one or two local volunteers to help, they will send another person or two along, and the few of you together can not only copy the whole cemetery more quicky, but do so within range of friendly voice and technical advice.

I find convalescence a dandy time in which to do index projects. You are still in the house because the 'flu bug has not left you perky enough to return to work for two or three more days, and you are getting on your spouse's nerves because you want something to do with yourself. That is the time to get your scissors and some papers and cut out several hundred — no, not paper dolls — small slips of paper. Then, take some history book or list of names and index it or them. To my knowledge, no one has yet indexed the Stewiacke centennial book. If they have done so, the results have not been made public or at least not announced far and wide. Most of the volumes of the **Collections** of the N.S. Historical Society have never been thoroughly indexed. Anyone who is literate, has the time and ambition, can help everyone if they were to do an index project and share the results by filing them in the P.A.N.S. or the local library and by notifying the **Genealogical Association** that such-and-such has been indexed and put on file in this archives or that library.

You may or may not realize it, but publication of anything historical in Nova Scotia is a precarious gamble at best. Few local histories make money unless they have government grants to help in their publication. The local historical groups and ·the Genealogical Association all function on subsistence amounts of money. They depend in the last analysis on local volunteers for work, funds, and would for the most part disappear or sink into insignificance were it not for such help. You can be a helper by doing something to further the study of history and genealogy in your community or congregation or county. Join or help to start a historical and/or a genealogical association in your area.

If someone brings out a local history book or a collection of family trees, or wants to assemble old pictures of your community, offer to help by subscribing for a copy. I own several dozen books on the history of Nova Scotia and would go so far as to say that half of them have no intrinsic interest for me, but I believe that it is important that such books be written and published. Therefore, each year I buy a few new publications out of a sense that I am encouraging something that is good for me and good for Nova Scotia. Some books are really well written and involve the reader from the first page. Douglas Eagles and the late Rev. Angus Johnston, for example, have the facility of attracting the reader the keeping his interest, although I doubt that I can tell you what these two local historians have in common, if anything. Other authors may not be blessed with the same ability to interest their potential readers, but we put them on our shelves for their reference value, and, as I have said, rather as an act of Nova Scotia piety.

Genealogy in the Classroom

With the topical interest that family research is enjoying, it will occur to many teachers that doing a family tree would make a good project for their pupils. And so it will, if you plan it carefully. This brief section does not tell you step-by-step what to do, but it should give you a few ideas about the possibilities and limitations of such a concept.

There are many excellent reasons why doing a family tree is sound project work. Doing such a project will develop in a pupil a sense of family and community, and an interest in and identification with the past. It will teach concepts of time and place, and is individual enough to prevent copying, either from other pupils or from encyclopedias, two of the deadliest enemies to project work. Historically speaking, such work will teach pupils what their textbooks do not: that there are limits to what is known or can be known about the past. Pupils can and should develop skills of selecting and evaluating evidence; of deductive reasoning, of conducting interviews; and of planning and executing a complex project having several phases.

Admittedly, then, it is a good idea. What should you as a teacher look out for? First of all, never give tracing of family trees as a project to ALL students, unless you know that there are no families where adoption, illegitimacy or scandal will produce hostile reactions to any research project. Pupils should be given an alternative project of trying to trace the ancestry of a friend or relative. For instance, if the pupil is illegitimate, it might still be possible to trace (a) a mother's family tree, or (b) the premier's ancestry, or (c) the queen's ancestry.

Secondly, no teacher has any business giving such an assignment unless and until he or she has personally worked one through, so that they know experientially what is involved. Archives and libraries in Nova Scotia become choked periodically with pupils sent to do genealogy or other historical projects. Many of these pupils have been sent by teachers who have either never visited the records repositories or who have not prepared the pupils for using such places. This gets the teacher and the school a bad reputation, makes pests of the children, and makes the librarians and research assistants a little less helpful to the next flood of unprepared or semi-prepared pupils to be launched at them.

The concept should NOT be competitive. Every family cannot readily be traced back as far as every other. One family may have had a professional genealogist work on theirs and go back to 1690. The next family may be unsure of where to go before mom's grandmother, born 1875. It may take more work to get the 1875 family back another generation than it will to go home and copy the numbers and names out of a professionally prepared article or book.

Teachers should allow children lots of time to carry out such an assignment. Children should go and get the full names, dates, and locations of their parents and grandparents first. Then they can draw them into a chart, which the teacher can examine and evaluate. Then the pupils could take the chart and decide (perhaps with parental advice) which of the four grandparents to choose to follow back to **their** grandparents. The important thing is that the teacher keeps a check on progress. Long-term projects tend to lag if they are not monitored. The finished product could be taken to art class and there put down on a large chart. Those having more flair could decorate their charts with heraldic devices or a scene symbolic of the family history — e.g., a product of the family trades, such as apples, fish, logs, barrels, etc.

Such projects can have useful spinoffs for other projects. To give a few examples:

(1) Family History and Time Lines: Pupils find that one grandfather was born in 1901, and a grandmother was born in 1917; that dad's parents married in 1929 and mom's in 1939. Get pupils to find out what was happening at the time these family events were going on — e.g., 1901 — Queen Victoria dies; 1917 — Halifax Explosion; 1929 — Depression begins; 1939 — World War Two breaks out. Possibly a child for whom doing a family tree is touchy could be put to work assembling a year-by-year list of key events for 1875 to 1945 for use by the others in their family tree relationship to history. Pupils could try to learn what part, if any, their family members played in the big events of their day, or what effect the events had on the family: depression, wars, epidemics and explosions are obvious examples.

(2) Family History and Geography: Pupils find as many places in N.S. as they can in which family members lived or worked. They draw or trace a large map and locate those communities. Find out what industry prevailed in each place. Did the relatives fit the pattern directly? indirectly? not at all? This can be done by looking at ethnic or religious patterns of settlement also.

(3) Place Search — assembling pictures and/or directory facts about sites of former family homes. Visit the spot today, and write up a comparative description.

(4) Photo Gallery — Have pupils bring in and assemble a display of family portraits. Be sure the pictures have pupils' names on the back before making a collage. Pupils might have a lot of fun trying to guess whose relative is whose. Teacher can help by adding a half a dozen miscellaneous

old pictures to the group and encouraging others to bring in pictures. This would be good particularly with children who do not write well.

(5) Family Traditions — have pupils bring in stories of family customs, etc.

Heraldry

Many people trace their family tree for as far back as it seems practicable to go, and then seek to embellish the results. A skillful use of anecdote and oral tradition makes an interesting touch and holds the reader's attention. Some folks want to make a chart of the family tree and set it off by use of heraldic design.

Most of us do not have a family coat of arms nor can we prove conclusively our relationship to someone who does. This is no disgrace, of course, as possession of arms (being armigerous) was the prerogative of a social class not heavily represented among the emigrants who came to the shores of Nova Scotia.

In the absence of an hereditary right to arms there is only one alternative if you wish to have a personal coat of arms. That is to go through the not inexpensive procedure of having arms granted. For families living in Sir William Alexander's "New Scotland," areas such as Nova Scotia, the lawful authority for a grant of arms is the Court of the Lord Lyon, H.M. New Register House, Edinburgh EH1 3YT, Scotland. Inquiries will be given prompt, courteous and expert service should they write there.

Whatever you do decide, do not fall prey to organizations that promise to find your own coat of arms and "prove" you have a right to it, and undertake to do so at a fixed price. If you would like to have an ashtray with the "O'Brien Arms" or a whiskey glass adorned with the "Campbell Tartan" that is your affair. Just do not let anyone talk you into believing it is your personal shield or tartan.

Conclusion

At the going down of the sun the day is ended and whatever shall be the course of that day it shall be concluded. So, too, with this little book. I have, like the duelist, offered my fire. I must now, like a gentleman, be prepared to stand fire. It is my sincerest wish that this, the first published book dedicated exclusively to giving some guidance to genealogical research in Nova Scotia, will reach the hand and eye of those for whom it is intended. If you are a family historian or one who is thinking of getting involved with research into genealogy in Nova Scotia, this guide book was compiled and written with you in mind. I have tried to be as straight-forward as possible without pretending that the whole work of tracing a family is easy. It is nothing less than daunting for a novice to undertake to trace a family tree accurately, completely and well. However, because a carpenter can build the best fence, we do not say that he alone can build a fence. So with the family history. An expert could do it better and faster, but why should you not have the challenge and the fun and the frustrations, if you want them?

As you work you run into difficulties. You can surmount many of these by trying another approach, consulting with others, and perhaps looking again in this book to see if there is some other stone you have left unturned. If you work with your eyes and your ears and your mind open, with a cooperative spirit and enthusiasm, you can do quite a deal towards solving the riddle of your own origins. When you have gone as far as you can inside Nova Scotia you will want to search elsewhere, in Europe, the British Isles, the West Indies, the United States, or anywhere on earth. Guidebooks for Britain and Europe, Canada in general, and for the United States exist in fair numbers, so I have not made this book thick with advice pertaining to areas beyond Nova Scotia. Any modern library will have several general genealogy books from which you may choose. My purpose here here has been to introduce you to Nova Scotian genealogy, show you the principal secondary and primary sources, direct you to various books, articles, societies, publications, and sources of help. If you conclude with more knowledge than you began, the exercise has been worth your time, and the writing mine. Good luck as you do your family tree and family history!

INDEX OF SURNAMES

Note: Only genuine surnames are indexed; those used in fictitiou
are omitted.

126

Lawson 49, 56, 58
Leadbetter 49
LeBlanc 9, 46, 56, 58, 117, 119
Lee 49
Léger 46
Lent 58, 103
Leonard 49
Leslie 10, 118
Letson 57
Lewis 49, 103
Liddell 58
Lillis 49
Lincoln 49
Little 38, 57
Locke 38, 49, 57, 103
Lockhart 57
Lockwood 49
Lodge 57
Logan 38, 57, 90, 117
Lohnes 118
Longard 10
Longfellow 49
Longley 38, 49
Lord 38, 49
Lothrop 38, 58
Loughery 38
Loveless 57
Lovett 49, 57
Lowe 44
Lusby 57
Lyde 49
Lyon 57
Lyons 57
McAlpine 70
MacAulay 38, 57, 119
McCabe 46
McCombie 57
McCulloch 9
McCurdy 38, 57
McDaniel 72
MacDonald 38, 44, 57, 58, 117, 118, 119
MacDougall 57, 118
MacDuffie 38
MaEachern 118

McEwan 38, 57
MacFarlane 57, 82
McGill 70
McGillivray 38, 57, 117
McGray 49, 57
MacInnes 57
McInnis 117
MacIntosh 38, 57
McIntyre 117
McIsaac 113, 117
MacIvor 38, 57
MacKay 38, 46, 47, 57, 70, 83, 117, 118, 119
McKean 49, 58, 117
MacKenzie 39, 44, 57, 70, 117, 118, 119
McKevers 57
McKim 57, 91
MacKinnon 39, 57, 103 117, 118
McKitchen 84
McLaughlin 82
MacLean 7, 39, 57, 117, 118, 119
McLellan 44, 118
McLennan 47
MacLeod 57, 90, 117, 118, 119
McMikel 84
McMillan 57
McNab 57, 112
McNeil 57, 117, 119
McNutt 39, 44, 57
McPherson 39, 57, 117
MacQuarrie 47
McRae 39, 119
Mabey 57
Macy 49
Manette 39
Mann 57
Manning 57
Marchand 119
Marshall 44, 117
Marsters 57
Martell 57, 119
Martin 57

Mascarene 49
Mason 49, 57
Matheson 57
Maxner 47
Maxwell 39, 57
Mayer 39
Mayet 39
Mayhew 49
Mayo 49
Melanson 47, 57, 117
Melvin 39, 49
Merriam 49
Merrick 49
Miller 39, 49, 57, 58
Millett 57
Mills 117
Minard 118
Miner 39
Minns 49, 58
Minot 49
Mitchell 49, 71
Mombourquette 119
Montgomery 57
Moore 49, 57
Moorhead 49
Morash 57
Morehouse 39
Morgan 49, 57
Morris 47, 49, 57
Morrissey 113
Morrison 49, 117, 119
Morrow 39, 57
Morse 39, 57, 117
Morton 49, 57
Moser 118
Mosher 39, 49, 118
Moulton 49
Muir 70
Mumford 49
Munroe 57
Murdoch 57
Murphy 39, 113, 118
Murrant 57
Murray 39, 49, 83, 118
Mutch 39
Nash 83, 84
Neaves 71

SUBJECT INDEX

THE AUTHOR

Terrence Michael Punch is a Nova Scotian of many ethnic origins, who was educated at St. Mary's and Dalhousie Universities and holds graduate degrees from both. He is author of numerous articles on local history and genealogy, and founding Chairman of the Genealogical Association of Nova Scotia, a former editor of the *Genealogical Newsletter,* and Contributing Editor to *Canadian Genealogist* in Toronto.

Mr. Punch is a Life Fellow of the Royal Society of Antiquaries of Ireland, a Fellow of the Royal Nova Scotia Historical Society, Vice President of both the Royal Nova Scotia Historical Society and the Charitable Irish Society of Halifax. He was formerly executive secretary of the Federation of Nova Scotia Heritage. He is a Director of the Altantic Canada Institute, and has lectured in the Atlantic Canada Studies programme at St. Mary's University.

He has compiled guides to cemeteries and various other records, and has researched and published the genealogies of the Tobin, Howe, Prescott, Thompson, West, Beamish and Fultz families. His historical works on the Dutch Village area won a first and a second prize in two contests sponsored by the Nova Scotia branch of the Writer's Federation of Nova Scotia. Both prize-winning articles and all the genealogies were published in the *Nova Scotia Historical Quarterly* or its successor, the *Nova Scotia Historical Review.*

In Irish studies, Mr. Punch has published *Some Sons of Erin in Nova Scotia* (Petheric), *Irish Halifax: the Immigrant Generation, 1815-1859* (St. Mary's University, and *Aspects of Irish Halifax at Confederation* (Ethnic Identity Conference Papers), and many articles.

He has prepared two guides to early newspapers in Nova Scotia, entitled *Nova Scotia Vital Statistics in Newspapers, 1769-1812* and *1813-1822,* and is now compiling a marriage guide for 1769-1841 and a study of eighteenth-century German settlement in Nova Scotia, as well as a guide to Montbéliardian families in Nova Scotia. This book, *Genealogical Research in Nova Scotia,* represents two decades of experience in the field of genealogy in Nova Scotia. It was given honourable mention in the 1979 Evelyn Richardson Awards. This is its third edition in five years.

Printed in Canada